To my favorite agent fate
Mrs God Richly B
you as you
read my :)

[signature]

MICAH
7:8

READ HOW GRACE CONQUERS

RECYCLED BY GRACE

One man's journey through life's struggles, hurts and hang-ups.

Shane West

Recycled by Grace
One man's journey through life's struggles, hurts and hang-ups.

Copyright © 2009 Shane West
www.shanewest.com

Published by Bounce Back Publishing

All rights reserved. No part of this book may be reproduced or transmitted in any form or by any means, electronic or mechanical, including photocopying, recording or by any other information storage and retrieval system, without written permission from Bounce Back Publishing
1050 Glenbrook Way 480, Hendersonville, TN 37075
www.bouncebackpublishing.com

ISBN: 978-0-615-34764-6
Printed in the United States

Book Cover Design by Jason Booker
Book Interior Design by www.KarrieRoss.com

First Edition 2010

DEDICATION

I would like to dedicate this book in four quarters.

To my Lord and Savior Jesus Christ,
    Thank you for finding the treasure beneath all the trash and for seeing not what I was, but what I could be. If it had not been for your love and grace on November 5, 1987 my life would have had a tragic end.

To my beautiful wife Dana,
    Outside of my decision to serve God, the decision to ask you to be my wife was the best decision I ever made. Over the past 20 years you have been there for me at times when nobody else was. Thank you for the unconditional love that you have shown to me, and for believing in me during the times that I could not believe in myself. While I reflected back on my life as I wrote this book, I once again stood in awe that God would somehow allow a man like me to marry such a wonderful Christian like you!
    Dana, after all these years, I am honored to be "Faithfully Yours."

To my three sons, Dakota, Zane, and Shane II, I want you boys to know that you have made me the proudest father in the entire world. I see in each of you greatness and a God given destiny that shall surpass anything that I have ever done in this world. Learn from this book and please never make the same mistakes that your father made. I want to thank each of you for being who you are. The greatest joy that I have experienced in life was getting to know each of you!

With great honor I dedicate this book to you Dakota, and to you Zane, and to you Shane II, my "Mighty Men of God in the Making."

Last but not least I would like to dedicate this book to Terry in Texas.

God gave me such a love for you. Beyond anything that the natural eye could see or the hand could hold onto. My life was changed when our paths crossed. Whether that change is viewed by many as good or judged by some to be bad, only our Heavenly Father knows. I miss you being in my life. If only your confidence in me could one day be "Recycled by Grace."

PREFACE

I know this corner. It's Teilman and Garland Avenue, a place where I have been thrown out by my family because of the monster that I have become. Let's be quiet though so we do not awaken the neighbors, they always start to stir around this time during the week; many because of their jobs, some simply because they are older and the older you get the less sleep you desire. Man, they wake up earlier than the roosters…no roosters here though on this city street corner, but old folks are still stirring just the same. You may want to know why I am asking you to sit here with me and why we are in fact at this street corner on November 2, 3, or is it November 4? Lord only knows - I don't because I have been up for days.

Well you see my mother goes to work as a waitress at around 5:45 am, six days every week. She has been single for many years and has had to raise us kids all alone, except for some help that some boyfriends gave now and then.

I am now 21 and have always known my mother as a hard-working waitress…she leaves though really early like this and that's when I can sneak back into the house through the garage…I can't go in when she is there because she has kicked me out of the house. No please, don't look that way like she's a bad mother, she's not.

In fact, all of the blame goes on me; I have stolen from her, lied to her and disappointed her time after time. She just got to the place that she could not stand the losses anymore and asked me to leave…in fact, she told me I could come back if I got myself straight...man, what are the chances of that, I would have a better shot at winning the lottery, right?

Yeah, she will be leaving shortly and we can sneak back into the house to get just a few hours of sleep...man I have been strung out for days...three, maybe four days of no sleep, living on the streets. I remember last night I slept in an alley not far from here using some cardboard that had been broken down to recycle as my only covers. Just a couple of days ago, I had so much cocaine in my system that my muscles would no longer work. I couldn't stand or lift my arms. I thought I was going to die. I remember watching my chest, waiting to see my heart burst right out of my clothes. This is my life?

It's probably 35 to 36 degrees out here, and really foggy...man I am so tired; I have been in this fight of drug addiction since I was fourteen. Seems like the demon of cocaine has got me about whooped...my knees are weak, my body seems to be burning up with fever and all I want is to lie down and rest. Is there any such thing as solitude? Does peace really exist or is that just a word made up by the higher echelon of society? You know I am scared because I have been thinking over the past few days that my family, and even those that once called me a friend, and this entire world for that matter, would no doubt be better off without me. Maybe tonight I will end it all.

I know that my brother Steve keeps a gun hidden in that converted garage where I am going to lie down in just a few more minutes. I feel so beaten down, so weak, so punch drunk from life and addiction! WAIT, there walks my mother to her Cadillac, I can see that she is now getting in the car...ssshhhhhh listen there, it is the sound of her car starting. Mom is leaving in just a few more minutes...I wonder what she's thinking, is she thinking, "Where's Shane this morning?"

I wonder if she has wondered where her baby boy is staying, where is he sleeping, is he even alive? Is he ok? Is he dead?

PREFACE

Okay… there she goes, she drives away from the house and I make it to the little window that cannot stay locked and I open the window and crawl inside.

I lay down in that little garage just for a few minutes to get some rest, to feel some warmth, although not much, it is better than being exposed to the air. It has been days since I slept…my heart is beating so dang fast and hard…I am sweating, I am wondering why am I still alive…what have I done with my life?

I feel like the enemy of my soul has knocked me down, lower than I have ever been knocked down before! I am wondering should I stay down, should I call it quits, should I reach for that pistol and really end it today? I reach for the pistol that I have held many times before but I place it back down and tell myself that if my heart will just slow down enough to let me sleep, surely I will feel better, surely my life is not over and I begin to rest knowing that I cheated death once again. I do not give in to my thoughts; this addiction and bondage is kicking my butt but it looks like I will live to fight another day. I have no idea where I am headed, or what I am going to do with my life, but my day of grace, November 5, is in fact on the way!

So you see the first few days of November 1987 were pretty tough. I did not have a home to live in or a bed to sleep in. My mother had rented out the room that I had once called mine, renting it to my best friend Andy. I did not know what I was going to do. I had suffered so many losses and disappointments in my life. On November 4, 1987, I was 21, living on the streets and walking the back alleys of Fresno. By this time in my life I had been stolen from, robbed and abandoned, but isn't that what a thief comes to do? *To steal, kill, and destroy!*

My life had become trash, but it wasn't always going to be that way!

RECYCLED
BY
GRACE

CONTENTS

CHAPTER 1	Where It All Began	15
CHAPTER 2	Home Alone	27
CHAPTER 3	Growing Up Without a Father	33
CHAPTER 4	Great America, Here I Come	41
CHAPTER 5	Return to Sender	49
CHAPTER 6	The Gift That Just Kept On Giving	53
CHAPTER 7	If This Is All That Life Has, Life Sucks	63
CHAPTER 8	The Discovery of Crack Cocaine	71
CHAPTER 9	Memorial Day, 1984	79
CHAPTER 10	From Bad to Worse	83
CHAPTER 11	November 5 — Recycled By Grace	87
CHAPTER 12	My Recycled Life	107
CHAPTER 13	Kingdom Keys	113
CHAPTER 14	Closing Thoughts	125

CHAPTER 1

Where It All Began

Outside the wall of the old city of Jerusalem in 29AD, our world was forever changed. A Roman soldier took an amber-colored olive tree stake and nailed the hands and feet of whom he thought to be a criminal. Little did that soldier know he was piercing the flesh of God.

That hot April day in Palestine, the great Messiah, the one that was spoken of throughout the Old Testament, shed His own blood for our redemption. But going back in history, it can easily be seen that the disciples, and majority of believers for that point, did not truly understand the concept of pain. They had, no doubt, never really considered or contemplated the phrase that would be coined hundreds of years later that simply said, "What doesn't kill you only makes you stronger." No, the disciples really did not understand pain in relationship with Christ, the Chosen One, their Messiah.

Pain's meaning was hidden from them, and they did not know what He was talking about many times as Christ made references and alluded to pain. They wanted and expected a Messiah who would come and free them from their pain, not a Messiah who would Himself go through pain and agony, shame and reproach. It's a testimony to how we tend to find what we're looking for, is it not? The thing that we expect to see; it's a testimony to our capacity to do that, like these disciples who were orthodox Jews, knowing that Jews knew their scripture very well; they were completely unaware of the prophecies that said the Messiah would suffer. They were very aware of the prophecies about the Messiah reigning victorious. They wanted to see those, so they saw those, all the time being blind to the other ones that dealt with any promise of pain or misfortune. They weren't so keen on seeing the prophecies about the Messiah suffering and so those just went over their head; for example, Isaiah 53, and prophesy that so often spoke of pain.

So Jesus is there telling them, before I reign in power there's going to be this suffering, and they just didn't have a clue to what He was talking about.

Now why did Jesus have to go to Jerusalem and suffer? The answer, of course, is that He did so because it was the only way of freeing us from the devil's domain, from the oppression of the powers of darkness. It was the only way to bring about the complete reconciliation between God and fallen man, the relief and forgiveness of our sin; and it was the only way that God could get us freed to live with Him for all eternity.

And the reason why God was keen on doing that was because of His unconditional love for us. Insomuch that the Bible says that as excruciating, as nightmarish, as painful as Calvary was, Jesus still considered it joy to go through it in order to be with us.

WHERE IT ALL BEGAN

> *Having our eyes fixed on Jesus, the guide and end of our faith, who went through the pains of the cross, not caring for the shame, because of the joy which was before him.*
>
> (Hebrews 12:2)

For the joy that was set before Him? There was no joy in being tortured, mocked, spit upon and then crucified. Jesus Himself sweat drops of blood as He faced the prospect of being handed over to experience the enemies' wrath and all the things He was going to go through with the sin of the world being put upon Him. *There's no joy in that,* **or is there?**

The joy is in what it accomplished, and what it accomplished was reconciling us to the Father and opening up the way for us to live with Him throughout Eternity.

Never think for a moment that you are a bother to God.

Sometimes people do nice things for you, but you know that often we are an inconvenience to them, and maybe they'll let you know that by saying, "All right, I'll do it." There's no "all right, I'll do it" in God. It gave God joy to do what He did to be reconciled to us.

That draws our attention to a Kingdom principle. It's called the Calvary principle, aud it is this: *to get to the joy you have to go through the suffering.* Most things in life that bring joy and fullness of life require that we suffer on the way to getting there.

We must embrace the pain on the way to getting there. Is it not the mother that testifies about the great agony of child birth, and the perils often seen in labor? But quickly that pain that was experienced in labor is replaced by such great joy when that newborn baby is placed in her arms for the first time. No doubt she then reflects back, and determines that the joy of looking into that newborn's eyes for the very first time is greater than the pain she experienced in her body. So if we can get a glimpse of the reward, can we not then, find a way of embracing the hurts, realizing that it is through life's hurts and pains that often later bring great joy?

Embracing the pain for me has come both long before I knew Christ, and even after meeting Him, but all of my life, all of my troubled nights and homeless days, through all of my addictions, hurts, and hang-ups, all of this was leading up to Shane West being *"Recycled by Grace."*

I was born July 25, 1966, into what I later discovered to be called by society "a dysfunctional home." It was a crazy home with commonly witnessed exploits of alcoholism, drug addiction, divorce and domestic violence; roles were being played out so very well by my parents.

I do not remember much about a childhood, nor do I remember much about my younger years. I do remember however, at the age of five, my father putting me on his lap, looking into my eyes saying, "Sweetheart, your mother and I are going to walk our separate ways." I could never understand how a father could walk out and turn his back on a five-year-old son, leaving us all alone. Due to alcoholism, a bar-room scene, a jukebox, a dance floor, and of course another woman (ironically bearing the same name as my mother), my father left my mother and I. One of my greatest memories as a young boy is the fact that I do not really have many memories of being a young boy! As a single parent, my mother raised me, but many times her working the graveyard shift (as a waitress, for over 51 years) forced me to live with baby sitters and different family members. I remember

WHERE IT ALL BEGAN

Mom so often, when she would be home, looking into my eyes and saying, "You're going to grow up to be just like your father, LOOK AT YOU, Shane! You look just like him, you talk like him and you walk like him. Yeah you will grow up to be a loser just like him! You're going to be an alcoholic."

And that's what I remember hearing as I grew up. Just hearing the words of negativity and hearing the words that alcoholism would control my life, as it had my father's life, shook me to the very core at a very early age. I was constantly reminded that I looked just like my father and so I would grow up to be just like my father, right?

That is why now, raising three sons of my own, ages ten, nine, and five, I have committed to constantly, on a daily basis, speak positive words into their lives, thinking, if those negative words scarred my emotions while I was at an early age in life, what more could be done with positive words and encouragement for my sons to hear, embrace, and apply at the early ages of their lives? I simply have made it a point to speak good things, and God things, breaking all generational curses that I learned had been handed down to me. I have made a commitment and a concentrated daily effort, reminding my three sons of their excellence, their destiny, their high calling in Christ, as well as my unconditional love and respect for them.

If you could approach any of these "sons of thunder" and casually ask them, "What are you, Dakota? What are you, Zane? What are you, Baby Shane?" with a sound of assurance and confidence, they each would reply, "I am a mighty man of God in the making."

Why? Reflecting back I can see how words of negativity and hurt, somewhat chartered my course in life. If I lived out that which was spoken over me, why shouldn't my sons live out what is spoken over them…positive, loving, affirming words of daily encouragement? I know that this will make a difference in each of their lives. I have decided wholeheartedly to break each and every generational curse in my life, and the lives of those around me. Try it today, it's not too late, start speaking over people's lives in a positive manner.

You would be utterly shocked to hear the things that I have heard in churches and in parents' conversations with their children. Mind you, these are churchgoers, church leaders, and members of a faith based community, speaking words to their children like "shut up–quit being stupid–you're such an idiot–what are you, retarded?" These words should *NEVER* be spoken over our children! We must break the generational curses that the enemy has strategically placed in our family's lives, our homes, our children, their children, so forth and so on. Breaking these curses is non-negotiable; you've got to break the domino effect of generational curses to fulfill Kingdom impact, to break the domino effect falling on generation to generation.

You know what dominoes are. You push one down and they're all in a line, and one pushes down another, which pushes down another, which pushes down another. Many family systems are just like that. In fact, I believe that to a certain degree, most family systems are that way. Things get passed on from generation to generation, parent to child. It becomes the parent who hands it down and gives it to the child, it then becomes that child that grows and becomes a parent who gives it to his or her child, and it goes on and on and on. Dysfunction, habits, character flaws and sin get handed down.

Now here's how it works. You've heard this slogan perhaps — "Wounded people wound other people." This proves to be the case many times. Parents tend to wound their kids, who become wounded parents who wound their kids, who become wounded

WHERE IT ALL BEGAN

parents who wound their kids, and the dominoes just keep on falling from one generation to another.

If you're going to be a Kingdom Driven Parent, you've got to cleanse and purge your heart and break the domino curses that you've inherited, as being born into a family system.

My mother, I'll share about her throughout this book, was abusive in terms of her forms of punishment, relatively normal otherwise, but she would snap when she got angry, and some very sick things happened, and I just thought she was crazy and hated me growing up. But when I got older; I learned that, in fact, that's exactly how she was punished by her mother, and exactly how her mother was punished by her mother, and so on and so on. Who really knows how long ago that got started? Later in my life I discovered that my grandfather died while my father was just a young boy, so my father never had an example or a positive pattern to draw from.

Parental patterns tend to be repeated from one generation to another, for better or worse.

Consider any sex abuser that you might know, or one that you have perhaps read about, the odds are that they were themselves sexually abused. There's not a formula here, there's always exceptions to the rule, but it is more likely than not that they themselves were abused. Take a person who is prone toward violence toward their kids and abusive toward their kids. It's more likely than not that they themselves were victims of violence. Take parents who tend to abandon their kids, or get emotionally distant from their kids. It's more likely than not that that's exactly how their parents were towards them. There's a family that I know where there's at least three generations of this. **Parental patterns tend to be passed down.**

The dominoes keep on falling, and the interesting, yet sad thing, is most of the people who carry on the curse of the generational dominoes, if the truth were to be known, most of them really hate and despise it. They say, "I can't keep doing this, I have got to stop, why do I, why does this happen in my life and in every generation, I just can't seem to stop." They don't like what they're doing, yet they find that they can't help it. It feels like instinct to them. They can't see any other solutions. What's happening is the curse is being handed down. The domino effect is happening in our families, and there are some that are part of a domino chain of shame. Others are part of a domino chain, maybe, of sexual abuse or just of violence.

Some are a part of a domino chain of poor parenting skills, parents who have been distant and are non-affectionate, unable to show, speak, or demonstrate any love to others. Some a part of a domino chain of alcoholism, drug addiction, moral and sexual perversions, overeating, and the list goes on and on. Some are even a part of a domino chain where everything looks very good, but there are deep, dark secrets hidden. The curses tend to be handed down, but while you read this book, I believe that God is equipping you with the truth and ability to break every chain and curse that has been handed down and cast on upon you. Serve notice with me right now ... the curse is **BROKEN!**

My family became friends with a wonderful woman named Donna, who I met in Arkansas, and had the opportunity to minister to during a revival a few years ago. Donna wept one night as she described in detail how her family members had witnessed several suicides. A mother, an uncle, a sister, and other family members, just decided to "check out," she said. But with the help of God, Donna decided to forever *"Reverse That Curse"* and is doing well even today. Are there any curses that need reversing in your life?

Jesus Christ can reverse the curse for you as you read this book today!

WHERE IT ALL BEGAN

THE GRASS WAS GREENER ON THE OTHER SIDE

As a young boy, I was very regularly headed to hospitals, sometimes late at night, often in the early morning hours, due to my acute asthma. I would awake having severe asthma attacks many mornings at two, three o'clock, sometimes even four in the morning. My mother would cover me up with blankets and head towards the hospital, fighting fog and weather conditions, many times to get me to The Fresno Children's Hospital, where I would spend the night, or a week, or several weeks, usually in an oxygen tent, very weak.

There was a particular morning that my asthma had reached an all-time high, a very critical time, a critical hour, Mother driving hysterically down a foggy highway to get me to the hospital that was about a 45 minute drive from where we lived. This time my fever peaking at an ever so dangerous 105–106 degrees, refusing to go down even after many various medications were given.

This time, the asthma attack felt different, like a grown man with his large hands around my windpipe, or a heavy beast lying across my chest, a heavy weight that I could not get off my chest to find any relief to be able to breathe. As my mother carried me into the emergency room, we were met by nurses and physicians that quickly saw this young boy named Shane that was in dire need of medical attention, or at the least Divine intervention. Within minutes, they had lowered me into what appeared to be a stainless steel rugged-looking horse trough that had been filled nearly to the top with nothing but ice! As they dropped me into that ice, I remember feeling like I was on the verge of having muscle cramps and the charley horses were getting ready to run and pull at my calves and my legs. So cold, nothing but ice, and a few minutes later after an injection, my fever dropped to a manageable temperature.

My mother was later told that the ice bath saved my life! That particular hospital stay lasted for nearly three weeks and the doctors were trying to figure out a better way to treat my asthma or perhaps a change of meds would be required to stabilize and control this sickness. I remember while lying in the oxygen tent I had a few family members that came to see me; I remember how they looked through the bubble, Shane on the inside, family of Shane on the outside. I remember spending time that night just looking and thinking, listening to the oxygen source being used to pump oxygen into the little bubble and for the first time in my life I started feeling a great peace.

Now that I am a man reflecting back, the best way that I could put into words what I began to feel that night would be just before you go under anesthesia for surgery, you know the time just moments before, when you couldn't care less about what happens – your body often tingles. Often you can feel as the anesthesia begins to take effect, how peaceful one's body becomes. This is exactly how I began to feel, but there were no doctors in the room, no nurses — I do not even remember being on any IV drip at that time. I just simply began to look into the faces of my family members, and suddenly felt a great peace, an ease and calm, to all of my hurts, both physically and spiritually.

I felt a great calm that day that I had never felt before, nor have I ever felt since. I thought I was beginning to dream but that could not be possible, because I was still looking at a handful of people that were in my hospital room, but wait, I just realized that I am not looking to them now from my bed, but rather I am looking at them from above my bed, almost as if I were on the bottom of the ceiling looking down. I was looking at them

WHERE IT ALL BEGAN

outside of my own body, I felt so peaceful and calm…after just a few short moments of wishing that I could invite my family to come and go with me — but go? Go where? I did not know — but I did know that I was walking away from that setting of sickness and I was approaching another setting, a very warm peaceful setting. I saw very tall blades of grass, and grassy fields as far as my eyes could see. I thought, wait a minute I am very warm now, there is actually like sunshine patting me on my back.

That oxygen tent that I came out from was so very cold; I remember often thinking, *"If my asthma doesn't kill me the pneumonia I catch from this cold oxygen bubble surely will."*

But the place that I had just walked into was very warm, very radiant, and very peaceful. Seeing the tall blades of grass gently blowing in the wind from side to side, seeing the brightness of sky and warmth of its rays caused a great peace to be felt, and I just kept walking in the grass, running my hand through the grass and simply being warm and carefree. There were no hurts, no pains, no bad memories, no arguing, and no broken dreams from the past, or disappointment from broken promises made.

I am trying my dead-level best to express and describe this place to you, but even after 35 plus years, I find it hard to pen, type or speak the words. So very beautiful, such harmony and peace, no fear, just great sunshine and a soft-blowing wind moving the tall grass side to side. Hills upon hills as far as my eyes could see. Hills covered with flowers that had all of my favorite colors: blues, yellows, purples…but where had I gone? How did I get here? I don't have to leave this place, do I? I did not know it then but could it have been this place?

> *And the town has no need of the sun,*
> *or of the moon, to give it light:*
> *for the glory of God did make it light,*
> *and the light of it is the Lamb.*
> *(Revelation 21:23)*

    Moments later, the great warmth that I had been feeling with my heavenly experience vanished, and quickly I was once again shivering and cold inside that oxygen bubble, and once I recognized that I was back in my body, recognizing that I was not going to be able to stay in that wonderful place, I began to cry, I cried and my family as well as the nurses began asking if I was in pain or discomfort. The nurse would ask things like, "Do your lungs hurt, Shane? Do your legs hurt? Are they cramping again, Shane?" I wanted so bad to explain to them nothing is hurting except for my heart; wherever that place was I wanted to stay there forever. Well by the grace of God, someday I can return to the place that as a little boy I visited where the grass was truly greener on the other side!

CHAPTER 2

Home Alone

Even though I grew up around constant violence between my mother and father, the fighting was not limited to just them. Mother was a hard working lady, and just as much a hard fighting woman. She always had a very independent spirit and attitude when it came to others, and for the biggest part of my life, I remember her fighting with everyone around her. My mother was married at least five times that I know of, and from the time I was five, she always had a boyfriend "shacking up" with us.

The reason I say "hard-working" is because of the many hours that Mom spent working as a waitress in coffee shops around Fresno. For whatever reason, whether her age (I was born to a mother that had just turned 37 — she often told me that I was a mistake, seeing that she was going through the change of life AND on the birth control pill at the time of my conception), or whether it was just her preference, Mom mostly worked graveyard shifts as a waitress and was very well-respected among the younger women that worked around her.

Many times, her boyfriends would go in to see her at work and I was able to go in just to sit and watch her as she went from table to table, serving, pouring coffee, bringing several plates stacked on her arms; she could bring five or six plates at a time and serve those tables, many times for just a dollar or two, maybe three dollars. It was a small breakfast house here, or a rundown coffee shop, or truck stop there, so it was not a place that the ticket would ever be costly; therefore, the tips were never large but Mom was such a hard worker that she made those dollars add up. I don't know how she did it, but as she raised my brother and me, she always had money and was never broke. We always were able to have some food in the refrigerator and some cup of noodles in the cabinets. "Elaine the waitress" was who many customers asked for when coming to the restaurants and coffee shops that employed her. Reflecting back on Elaine the waitress, I see that through her hard work she was able to find a security and the ability not to have to ever depend upon a man again. The hurt that my father and others caused her, I believe, made my mother become bitter toward men in general.

I remember hearing her often argue and fight with not only my father, but her live-in boyfriends, saying, "I don't need you, I don't need any man; get your stuff and leave if you don't like it around here!" The crazy and sad thing is, that she even took that approach towards me, her youngest son, often screaming in a rage saying, "You can pack your bags too mister. If you don't like it around here, then just leave! I work hard to pay the bills, and if you don't like it around here pack your bags and leave. Get out, go find what bar your Dad is drunk at, and climb under the barstool with him."

She once threw a dime at me and told me to put it in my pocket so that when she kicked me out, I could call my drunken father. *(Phone calls were only a dime back then!)*

HOME ALONE

I remember one time after she spoke those words to me I screamed back to her and said, "Mom, I'm only seven, where can I go? I'm just a kid, how could you kick me out? You and Dad are the ones that had me; I never asked to be born."

Her hurtful reply was that if my father had not come home early one day, only to catch her before she left with a friend, she said, "I would have aborted you from the beginning, if I could have had my way." Then later, when Mom would begin to feel bad about the argument or hateful statements, she would come to me and promise to buy me something nice - a toy, some clothes, etc.

Through the adult years of my life, I myself have had to be careful, or I too will be just like my mother in many ways. If I begin to feel bad about myself, or am carrying guilt and shame, I will try to give something of monetary value to someone, thinking that this will make me feel better about myself. I cannot begin to count the watches that I have given away, or how much money I have wasted on others, in hopes of feeling better about myself. The dinners that have been bought, presents purchased, even recently giving a Hummer H2 away, and guess what, I felt great about giving, but it never made me feel better about myself.

Mom, you were a very hard-working woman, but what I wanted more than for you to buy me a toy, or a pair of shoes, was simply for you to come and hold me, hug me, love me and tell me that you love me.

It would have felt so awesome to have heard those words, but Shane never did.

A KNIFE IN THE BACK

I grew up in the presence of many other men, the boyfriends of my mother, most of whom she met through working at the coffee shops that she worked at; one in particular was an older man named Elliott, who was very kind. Although he was more of a grandfather figure in my eyes, I now look back and see that Elliott did his best to treat and help raise me like a son.

Remembering the many, many times as a sickly boy and often visiting the hospital for asthma, it was Elliott that would be there often with something that would cheer me up, something that would brighten my day. I never could understand how a stranger could be there, and my father is absent. There was a Thanksgiving in particular I remember the drunkenness and disorder that began; it started with a small wisecrack or joke and soon escalated to an all-out fight. I remember this time though, running outside and walking around our property just trying to escape the craziness, just trying to find somewhere where there was harmony and quiet to be found, searching over most of the five acres that we lived on. I am not sure how long I was outside that Thanksgiving Day but what I do remember is that it was cold in Fresno, and the popular thing in those days was goose down jackets. You know, the ones that are really puffy and if you draw the draw string after buttoning the buttons you would have an appearance of a buff, muscular man...man, I used to love those jackets. As I was walking under the driveway, I had been sitting in a car listening to the radio, probably seven or eight years old by this time, I saw Elliott walk around, and it looked like he was looking for me, and a few moments later he saw me sitting in the car. Elliott walked over to begin to talk with me. Elliott was not a drinker so he was the only sober person on the property,

HOME ALONE

and Elliott tried to console me - console me about my mother, console me about my father, console me about a bad Thanksgiving Day and when he finished talking as Elliott turned to walk away I could not believe my eyes.

To this day, if I would not have seen this for myself I would have trouble believing that this really happened. Elliott had a knife stuck in his back! There was a kitchen-sized steak knife that was dangling from his jacket; the back of his jacket actually had a knife hanging out of it. I thought, "Oh my God, Elliott is stabbed and doesn't know it!" So I screamed saying, "You got a knife in your back!!" The reason for my screaming was not only to try to help Elliott but the sobering sight of the reality of what my mother was capable of doing...*murder*, caused me to burst out with fear and disbelief! Elliott removed the jacket and to our surprise we both saw where the knife had entered into the jacket, but because of the large amount of "goose down feathers," the feathers acted as some type of a shield and the knife did not penetrate the skin! The knife was stuck into the jacket, into the goose down, but it had just nicked the skin.

Elliott later talked about how when he was walking out of the house, my mother, while yelling and screaming at him said, "Yeah, you belong outside also." and what he thought was a shove and a push on the back, or something thrown at him, was actually my mother, in her drunken rage, trying to stab this man.

So you see when my father and mother weren't having a knock-down drag-out good old-fashioned "Jerry Springer Show" fista cuff, my mother would be getting drunk on wine fighting with others. It seemed that my mother really wasn't happy unless she was fighting. I have met a lot of people like that in my lifetime. If everything is going well, or if there is smooth sailing in the waters of their life, they will spark something to get some drama sparked to break the calm. *Why do so many of us like storms?*

Something dangerous happened to me during this time of my life, just a young boy, and perhaps those who are reading this can relate somehow to what I am getting ready to say. While I was growing up with an abusive mother, I had a lot of pain, and there came a time in my life, that I remember, almost as if I documented it and perhaps I did, mentally…I made a promise to myself that my mother would never hurt me again. I will never allow my feelings to get hurt again — NEVER! I felt like I popped a major pain pill emotionally.

I'm not going to feel that pain anymore, no matter what she says, how hurtful her words may be, how many times she slaps my face, I will not feel her hurt any longer. And it amazes me that it worked. It actually worked. I never cried after that. No matter what she did, no matter what she said, no matter how hard she scratched my face, or threw me down, I never cried again!

The trouble with that type of numbing is that it winds up numbing everything, and you cut the emotion nervous system, and in doing so, you cut your ability and your capacity to feel much of anything. Now as a kid, I needed that. It helped me survive, but see there comes a time when that short-term solution has got to be let go and you've got to address the real problem.

You and I must face and embrace the pain, allowing God to do a work in our lives.

This is something that is not a quick fix, unlike what a lot of ministries would try to convince us to believe, as if just walking down the aisle or to an altar one time to repeat a prayer, maybe even feeling those emotional goose bumps from a service where the music and the emotions are quite stirring.

To enter into the joy of a fully alive, full-feeling, full-loving Kingdom, we must experience some junk in our lives, but still have emotions and love, entering into the joy that God desires each of us to have we must go through the pain.

CHAPTER 3

Growing Up Without a Father

I find it hard to express what I really felt during those youthful years that shaped my future. I do remember how things were just so messed up. I remember that I really used to dread holidays! You are probably thinking, "How can anyone dread a holiday?" Well in the environment that I was raised in and around, when holidays came, the law and troubles always came along with them. My family members would take these occasions to drink excessively and when that began it seemed that "all hell would break loose." My father would come over drunk and want to slap my mother or half-brother around, or anyone else that was present for that matter.

I remember nights when Mom would get a phone call from my drunken father, he would be screaming, yelling, and cursing, telling her that he was on his way over to cause her some hurt and pain, just like the hurt and pain that he had felt all night long, on a bar stool, with no home to go to, after closing hours. Soon after the phone call, I would see his car headlights or know that he was coming down the driveway so I would run and get into the bed, tuck myself in to give the appearance that I was asleep. I thought somehow if I could play like I was asleep, he would come and go faster; he would not scream at me or I could somehow possibly cause some conflict from happening, but more times than one, all that I would do is lay there and listen; once again, listen to my screaming mother scream at my father for "the abandonment," for the "broken promises and dreams" that they once shared, or for the "lack of child support."

Like many mothers in the day in which we live, my mother used me as a ransoming tool for the "child support" threatening that if the child support did not arrive, which most of the time it did not, I then would not be allowed to see my father! I wondered countless times, as I laid in bed pretending to be asleep, "Why does Dad come over drunk all the time, fighting with my mom, but will not come home, settle down and fight to be my Daddy?" I still remember always believing that somehow, someway, someday, it was all going to work out; it would all change, so for however long the fights and the arguments lasted I would try to find somewhere in my mind to escape to until this hellish night was over

THE FORD RANCHERO

I later found out, after I grew up, that my father was known in the bars of Fresno for two things: he was known for his wild fearless fights and his beat-up, ragged, fearless Ford Ranchero. Carl West drove a Ford Ranchero that I can remember seeing as if it was just parked outside my house yesterday. The reason the memory of that Ranchero has stuck in my mind for so long is because of the terror that I associated with that vehicle. I can still remember, as if it were yesterday, my father coming over drunk,

GROWING UP WITHOUT A FATHER

fighting and telling my mother that he was going to take me for the weekend. I had so many mixed emotions about that, I had a great hope to spend just a good weekend with my father, but he was so drunk I was scared to get in the car. My mother and he would fight over his drunkenness and if the conclusion was anything less than Carl West getting his way, many times he used the Ranchero as a weapon, driving over the yards both front and back, driving over potted plants — even my swing set was destroyed on one of his terror runs.

To this day I have not found a rollercoaster or a theme-park ride, a scary movie, a haunted house or anything for that matter that would put the fear and scare in me that his Ford Ranchero did. A matter of fact as I write this book, I can still recall what it was like, looking at my drunk father behind the steering wheel, ordering me to "get in" and hearing the passenger side door squeak as it would close, causing a shiver to run down my back, and a chill to grip my heart, not knowing whether or not this would or would not be my last ride.

The violence would continue through my early years, the insults, the threats, the slapping, shoving and hitting. Many times the police were called out to 4065 West Jensen Avenue because of, once again, a holiday gathering that turned violent. Whether that meant a verbal argument turned violent, a knife in the back of my mother's boyfriend, damaged property, a smashed swing set, or terror done by a drunk driver in a 1974 Ford Ranchero, tan in color with a stripe down the side. A memory that has long been branded into my mind was that of how often I would in fact be looking forward to weekend visitation from my father. When some money had been given to my mother, and there were no immediate plans to drink and to go out chasing women, my father would promise me to be there at the school right at time of dismissal so that we could begin our weekend together.

Due to the fact that my father never owned a home, neither did he lease, nor rent anywhere, he usually lived with my grandmother Flora in her 16x80 mobile home. My father and I would often spend weekends either in a motel or even in the back of that Ford Ranchero, parked somewhere for the night, with a makeshift mattress, and a couple of blankets. The discomfort of the surroundings did not bother me because I was with my hero — my father — but sad to say that many times when that hero was to pick me up at school, he would not show up. I had looked forward to it all week, even bragging to friends at school that the upcoming weekend was going to be so awesome, because I was going to spend it with my father.

Of course, I never would be truthful, letting the other kids really know that he and I would be staying in a rundown cheap motel, or camped out with sleeping bags in the bed of a Ranchero somewhere, but oh how I looked forward to seeing my dad.

One time in particular, I remember that it was a Friday and he was scheduled to pick me up. While playing baseball at recess with my friends, I remember being up to bat saying, "I am going to hit a home run for my dad; because we are going to be together this weekend!" A short time later, school was dismissed and I quickly ran to the area where the children got picked up by their parents but Dad was not there. I remember watching the children wave goodbye, as the school buses slowly pulled off the school campus, headed in the direction of the various neighborhoods, children laughing and smiling, happy for the weekend, but Dad was not there.

Now the buses had left and I was still waiting; my father was not there! Moments later, the school buses were returning from their routes and dropping the children off but while all the children got dropped off I was still waiting to be picked up! Now most of the teachers had left and as I was watching cars pull out of the parking lot, I remember my teacher asking, "Do you need a ride, Shane? Are you okay?" I quickly declined the ride and acted like everything was okay…but now with her and another teacher having left, all the cars were gone from the parking lot, and I was still waiting. The only car remaining was that of an old truck parked in the distance, which belonged to the school janitor. I saw him as he made his rounds cleaning the classrooms, even he himself asking, "Are you okay, son? Do you need a ride?" Now it had been over an hour that I had waited, then nearly two hours, with darkness creeping in, and I was getting scared: no teachers, no phone, no Father, why would my dad leave me stranded like that?

Why would he break his promises to me so often? I then saw the headlights pull into the school grounds alongside the fence where I waited and I could tell they were not the headlights of a Ranchero but rather the headlights from my mother's car. My mother would pull up and say, "Get in; your father is a no-show like he has always been." When crying and asking my mother where Dad was, she often would tell me that she didn't know, adding, "probably drunk on a bar stool somewhere." And like always the words in the back of my mind would play over and over again that I was to grow up to be just like him. Many times on the ride home I would vow to myself, promising to **NEVER** be like that man is!

A SLAP IN THE FACE

One Friday, Dad did in fact make it to West Park Elementary to pick me up from school. I remember when getting into his car he seemed troubled, he seemed frustrated, and when I began to inquire and ask about our weekend plans and what we were going to do, he told me that he had to make a quick stop, and then we would be able to spend the rest of the weekend together having fun! The stop that Dad made was to a two-bit bar called "The Astro," located directly off of Motel Drive in Fresno, a run-down hole in the wall bar, in an area known for its prostitution and drug sales.

I remembered one night overhearing my mother and father fighting, she began to make fun of him, and mocked him for being such a drunk. She began laughing at him because of an incident that had happened, where he had left several head of cattle that he had purchased, in the cattle trailer all night, while he danced and drank, causing most of them to get sick, trample one another and die. Mother was always so quick to bring out the fact that Dad was not a good businessman, recalling how he was so far behind in his bills, not able to purchase a home, nor pay child support. She didn't have to prove to me that he was a drunk; I was the one with him a lot of times while he was on the barstools. I, being just a child, would sit over in the area by where the pool tables were, watching him drink at the bar, and as the night went on he would get louder and louder, and I would be so ashamed and embarrassed that he was my father.

One night, I recall he called me from the bar and commanded me to walk over to the bar stools where he and some friends were; he then threw some change down on the floor — I believe looking back it was about 65 cents. He then shouted, "Go get your Dad a pack of cigarettes." I picked up the change and went over to the vending machine to purchase that box of red Marlboro cigarettes that my dad liked. Quickly returning to the bar stool area, as if somehow I would gain his approval, I was met with laughter as I handed him the pack of cigarettes. My father, speaking in a drunk sarcastic voice, said, "See men,

I told you that boy of mine was worth something. He got his old man a pack of cigarettes."

He would never know in his lifetime what that did to me that night when I was just ten or eleven years old. To think that my only self-worth was being an errand boy to and from a vending machine toting a box of cigarettes to my drunken father.

In school, I had children teasing me because while I was young the school nurses and staff diagnosed me with a speech impediment, saying that I was having trouble making pronunciations in and out of the classrooms. I remember the children at my school gave me a nickname that I hated. They called me "Twitty," because of my speech impediment that would cause me to say "twitty-one," "twitty-two" when I would speak numbers in front of the class. Many times the classmates would laugh at me because of this speech problem, and the teacher defended me one day saying, "Don't laugh at Shane, there's a lot of people that cannot speak well in front of other people." (She had no idea what I would do so successfully in my life — speak in front of large crowds and congregations.)

A person that had a great impact upon me during this time was my grandmother Flora; she was my father's mother who was so soft and gentle to everyone in her family and to all of those that knew her. A caring and loving mother, often joked about, and called our "Mother Hen" because when Flora was around, all of the family knew that everything would be peaceful and secure; she would protect us like a mother hen protecting her chicks, and did I mention her cooking? The hamburger mixed in the white gravy over homemade biscuits, with large slices of crispy bacon, along with a glass of her cold iced tea, not just that readymade, quick-fix tea, but tea that had sat out in the sun for a couple of days — yeah, that's what I'm talking about, definitely better than what any local restaurant could offer! Some of the memories that I do feel fond about include my grandmother Flora.

Many times the entire family on my father's side would have a reunion at my Uncle Gary's large ranch house. Gary was a very hard-working, successful building contractor and owned a thriving construction company in Madera, a town just about 20 minutes north of Fresno. Ironically, my dad and our family were always the black sheep at these reunions, in a materialistic and worldly successful sense.

And even at that tender age I could see that I was walking in his footsteps.

Many years later, my father looked into my adult eyes and apologized for those days and nights; he said he was sorry for taking me into bars and for all of those days he abandoned me at school. He told me how sorry he was for abandoning me those Friday afternoons, and while apologizing with tears in his eyes my father said, "Son, I am so sorry, your father is an alcoholic and I have done so much that I am sorry for." By this time I was a man myself and I thought, "Dad, these were times that we will never be able to get back, I forgive you Dad, but the hurt will always be there!"

CHAPTER 4

Great America, Here I Come

I was about nine or ten when I got the bad news. My mother approached me and began to tell me that because she had to work so hard as a single parent, my aunt and uncle had agreed to let me come live with them in Santa Clara, California. When I spoke to them, they began to say how excited they were to have me come to live with them, and how they felt that they could make my life so much better, giving me the stability that every young boy really needs.

My uncle, at that time, owned a golf club repair shop on a golf course that sat directly across from the Great America Theme Park. My aunt and uncle's home was down the street from the theme park, and they told me that they had purchased me a season pass so that every weekend I could go to Great America. Excited about the thought of living directly across from Great America, yet so curious as to why this would be happening, now I was faced with the fact that not only was it my father who apparently did not want to live with me or raise me, but now I saw that even my mother wanted to get away, give me away, pawn me off so that she could be set free of me. "What did I do?" I thought. I continually asked myself, "What could I have done different or better? Could I have made people around me love me more? I am only nine or ten years old." I thought, "Mom, if I need to be better I will, if I need to help you around the house I will. I love the thought of living across from Great America and all but I am leaving my mother and if my father could not 'show up to pick me up,' spending time with me on weekends, us living in the same town so close together, how in the world would he ever 'show up to pick me up' four hours away?"

But you see my feelings did not count in this decision; the decision had already been made. *I was just being notified of the decision.*

My bags soon after were packed and I remember the drive to Santa Clara. Yes, I headed to live right across the street from Great America!

BEING NORMAL FEELS GREAT

Just a few days after arriving in Santa Clara, I was amazed to find a life of what appeared to be normal; normality was something that I had never known.

To me normality included things like:
a. A regular schedule.
b. Home-cooked meals that offered somewhat of a schedule, i.e., breakfast, lunch and dinner.
c. No drunkenness.
d. No screaming.
e. No "knives in the back."

GREAT AMERICA, HERE I COME

    f. A simple conversation like "How was your day at school, Shane?" or "Did you bring your report card home today, Shane?"
    g. My own bed and bedroom that I could keep clean and feel safe in knowing that nobody was going to come over and cause havoc.
    h. Overall love and support, with discipline and responsibility.

The above-mentioned things were something that I had never known until moving right across from Great America. My days were good during this season of my life. I remember catching the school bus and going to school, making new friends and overall just living a normal life.

I began to really love and appreciate my aunt and uncle for what they had done for me at this time in my life. I mean, to take in a ten year old and treat him with love and respect like they did made a huge impression on my life.

After awhile, I really began to love my life; I loved the fact that my home was safe, my school work was being monitored, I was being mentored into a young man, and most of all I found something else.

I FOUND MY THING

As I had mentioned, my uncle did golf club repair and also customized golf club design and worked for many of the leading pros of that day. If you looked at any given Sunday at the leader boards for the golf tournaments that were being televised, nine times out of ten the golfer that was in the lead and the others making a run for the lead were professionals that were using either my uncle's clubs or he at the very least had done club repair for the majority of them. His golf club repair shop was located directly on the course named Fairway Glen Golf Course, a public golf course that was constantly busy and one that I learned to love and adore.

My aunt and uncle being in the golf business introduced me to what I believe is without doubt the greatest game ever played; it is a game that cannot really be mastered, but oh, the fun in trying.

At the age of ten, I was introduced to this great game and it soon after consumed my life. I literally lived to play golf! I would come home from school at around four o'clock and head right to the golf course to hit a couple of large buckets of practice range balls and then play at least 18 holes, sometimes squeezing 27 holes in, depending upon the daylight savings standard. I would practice until after dark and often use the property lights located on telephone poles as my light to try to master my sand shots, chipping, or putting stroke.

One day after hitting some range balls and practicing, I walked into the shop where my aunt worked behind the counter and I remember saying, "I found my thing!"

I began to travel a little bit playing in junior golf tournaments, winning some for my age division and really feeling great about my life and who Shane West was becoming. I remember hearing about this young kid that was amazing on the links. When watching him, I personally thought he looked stuck up and he really had to be, to call himself a "Tiger." My uncle being in the custom golf club business, and me now living with him, led me to meet many stars of the game. Ben Crenshaw, Lee Trevino, Johnny Miller, John Cook, and Juan *"Chi-Chi"* Rodríguez were just a few of the men that I had met, most of them giving me golfing instructions and teaching me lessons of the game.

I cannot explain how it happened; I can only say that it did in fact happen. I found something that took my mind off some of the junk that I had been exposed to. When I would get on that golf course and smell the mowed grass and hear the birds chirping and many times watch the dew cover the ground and the closing of another day, I really knew I had found contentment, and what a great feeling to have.

Those around Shane West at the time said, "This boy eats, drinks, sleeps, dreams and lives for the game of golf!"

GOOD FEELING GONE

Even though it had only been two or three months since I had moved in with my aunt and uncle, I began to look to them as my rock, my fortress. These were the first examples of normalcy in my life and for that simple reason alone, they had become my heroes!

Just as a young boy being pulled out of a burning car or apartment finds such great admiration for the one that pulled him or her out and saved his or her life, this is how I felt.

*I felt that they had saved my life,
and for this they had become my heroes!*

That good feeling that I walked around with, that good feeling that I went to bed with, that good feeling that I had when I walked onto the tee box or practice range was quickly shattered!

One night while my aunt and uncle had friends over, one of the guests had asked to use the bathroom; of course my aunt had politely told him where he could find the guest bathroom and which hallway to walk down to get there, but moments later I myself had to use the restroom and when I expressed that to my aunt, she simply said, "You can just go use ours in our bedroom." My mind was shattered and confused when while in my aunt and uncle's bathroom, looking for tissue, I found in the cabinet under the sink, a stack of dirty magazines, magazines like I had never seen before! These magazines had pictures that I had never known, seen, or imagined could or would be taken of, men and women, doing what I had never known would or could be done! My world was shattered. As I looked though this huge stack of magazines, I felt dirty and awkward, but going against my conscience, I just kept looking. Now, for the sake of the reader, let me please say that these were not the magazines that one could easily find in a liquor store, or made available at gas stations, or grocery markets — these magazines were the kind that were hard core, harder to get, and much more explicit than the *Playboy* or *Hustler* that one could purchase in public. That first discovery in that bathroom that day led me to sneak around every opportunity that I had to look at these magazines. I would sneak home from the golf course while my aunt and uncle were working to check out the latest issues that my uncle had brought home.

I remember completely losing the hero impression that I had for my uncle.

Why would he buy these things? Now I know that I am looking and lusting just as any young boy would no doubt do, but why would a married man look at such dirty, filthy, perverted images when he had such a loving wife and family? I cannot say that in the later years of my life that I have ever struggled with "addiction to pornography." There have been other vices and addictions that have tried to attach themselves to me like a leech, but pornography has not been one of them. Not that my vices, struggles and addictions have been any better or less sinful; please understand that in this book I am sharing enough ugliness about the person that I was before Christ that if I did or had a problem I would discuss it in these writings. I would have no reason not to; I really have nothing to lose. I guess I was just fortunate in not having addictions once I was away from them.

Please understand that at the age of ten, I had never had the "talk" about the "birds and the bees" with any parental figure so when seeing these graphic images I totally saw women in a different light. I believe that later on in my teenage years the enemy used that seed that was planted concerning the low-worth image that I had embedded into my mind to cause me to have difficulties in relationships and truly caring for the opposite sex. I saw them as a possession and not as the valued person that God designed and created them to be. Something happened there in that discovery of the "hidden stack" under the bathroom sink in the cabinet — something bad happened. I not only felt so dirty, but I also felt so bitter; I lost my heroes that had walked into my life and gave me something good!

You may ask, "Why do you say heroes in a plural term? Were these not your uncle's magazines? Was it not your uncle that had the problem?" My answer is simply this, I lost respect for my uncle because I now thought that he was dirty, and I lost respect for my aunt because of her allowance of that filth in her home. I realize how so very good they were to me but I felt that they had pulled me out of a terrible environment only to throw me into a sick, deviated world of raunchy pornography. After that experience, I viewed women differently. When I would see attractive women in a store, mall, restaurant, whoever, wherever – I would wonder to myself, "Is she one of those women?"

I began to think that all women had that dark nature and maybe my aunt also had that dark nature, but she just grew older and perhaps was no longer like that. Pornography has a way of changing the perception of how one views women in general.

While there are many ways that pornography harms children, I realize that every child who views pornography will not necessarily be affected and, at worst, traumatized in the same way. The effects of pornography are progressive and addictive for many people. Just as every person who takes a drink does not automatically become an alcoholic, every child who is exposed to pornography does not automatically become a sexual deviant or sex addict.

Yet, according to one study, early exposure (under 14 years of age) to pornography is related to greater involvement in deviant sexual practice, particularly rape.

Slightly more than one-third of the child molesters and rapists in this study claimed to have at least occasionally been incited to commit an offense by exposure to pornography.

Among the child molesters incited, the study reported that 53 percent of them deliberately used the stimuli of pornography as they prepared to offend.

W. L. Marshall, "The Use of Sexually Explicit Stimuli by Rapists, Child Molesters, and Non offenders," The Journal of Sex Research 25, no.2 (May 1988): 267–88.

CHAPTER 5

Return to Sender

I am not sure if my aunt and uncle ever figured out what was going on. I do feel that they probably did, seeing that I no doubt failed to arrange the magazines like my uncle had them or perhaps they found one in a defiant hiding place one time or another. For whatever reason they called me to the kitchen table a couple months after my discovery, to share with me the news that I would be moving back to Fresno. They said they thought it best that I go back and live with my mother. Basically, they did not want to raise me any longer!

When hearing this announcement that I was to move again and take residence with my mother, who at this time, was living in the projects, still working as a waitress, trying to get on her feet, I had so many bad feelings and thoughts that circled my mind. Thoughts of once again feeling abandoned, thoughts that I had long forgot having, thoughts that said, "Shane it has to be you - nobody wants you." Something happened in the mind and spirit during that season of my life. I felt that I was broken down. The time, the endless hours I had spent getting fairly good at the game of golf, my passion, my love, my life, the game of golf, the family setting, the normalcy in living, all of this was to be taken away simply because my aunt and uncle say it would be best for me. Best for me or most convenient for them?

I must say that for many years I struggled with what happened; I felt that my hopes and dreams had been led along like that workhorse or mule chasing after the carrot that dangles in front of him. So close yet so far away, but one more step and I will be there; one more step and I will gain happiness; one more step and I will succeed, only to find that no matter how many steps you take, you can never reach that carrot. It is only placed there by another to get something out of you, some type of satisfaction, and the haunting reality was trying to set in once again. "Your father, Shane, left because you were not worth fighting for; your mother treated you the way that she did because of the bad son you were; your aunt and uncle do not want you living with them any longer because they loved you at first but the more time they spent with you the more they discovered you and the more the discovered you the more they realized that they did not like you."

"Shane, it has to be you. **You are so messed up, Shane, nobody wants you!**"

A few days after they told me the news that I was being returned to sender, I began to get my personal belongings together and organized. I remember crying and sobbing as I went through the drawers where my socks and t-shirts lay folded. I remember the feeling of packing up my stuff, asking myself, "Am I a drifter? Will I be like a vagabond all my life?"

> *"Am I really going to grow up to be like my father, a man without a home?"*

Soon after, my uncle knocked on my bedroom door and told me that we were ready to head to Fresno so they could drop me

RETURN TO SENDER

off. It seemed like it was so easy for them just to drop me off, almost like parents dropping their child off at a baby sitter that is trusted, knowing that in a few hours, the parents and child will be reunited, but this is not the case. They, in fact, were like the care giving, loving baby sitter giving me a better life, and now they were dropping me back off with my mother knowing all the time that we would not see each other anymore.

I remember thinking so hard on all the words and promises that were made to me; I kept running them through my mind, I kept getting even bitterer in regard to those magazines that were hidden under the sink. I thought, "Maybe I should bust him out right here in front of my aunt and my mother." Then the most hurtful thoughts came to my mind that kept saying, "I thought you guys said that you loved me, and were proud of me. You promised that you would be there for me. You promised to help me grow up to be a good young man. You said that we would have a great future together. You told me to fight hard for good grades, and so I did, and I got them; you told me to fight hard to become excellent at the game of golf, and so I did, won tournaments and was committed wholeheartedly to the sport; you told me to fight hard to get over any hard feelings that I had toward my mom and dad. I did fight hard I just never was able to win, was I?"

To my aunt and uncle, I want you to know that I did fight to be a good son to you; I did fight to do everything right, from my attitude, respect and my grades.

Yes, I fought hard to live strong and do the right thing; I fought so hard to stay with you, because somehow I know my life would have been so much better.

I thought that "we" were worth fighting for, and now here I am bruised, bloody, and broken and you aren't even breathing hard...guess I was the only one fighting!

CHAPTER 6

The Gift That Just Kept on Giving

At the age of 14, I remember a family member giving me a quarter gram of cocaine as a birthday present. That birthday present turned out to be a gift that "just kept giving" - giving me years of sorrowful nights and days spent in a prison that had no bars! I thought that if I were to make the choice to do cocaine, somehow I could escape the reality of my very bad childhood.

Somehow, I could escape the memories of hiding under the covers when a drunken father came over to the house and began to physically abuse my mother and half-brother (and anyone else living in the house with us, for that matter).

I thought that I would be able to escape all of the taunting words of my mother and the physical and verbal abuse of a dysfunctional family. I thought by simply doing a few lines of cocaine, I could become a happy young boy and experience "my escape." Yes, I could actually escape the reality of my life up this point.

Wow, what a setup of the enemy!

I do want to make it very clear though, I do not blame this experience and the following pages of hardships to how I was raised, who my father and mother were or were not, nor do I blame the dysfunctional setting in which I grew up in. I simply made the terribly wrong decision to try getting high. I made that choice. I'm the one responsible, and I am the ultimate person to blame in this story. Looking back now, I see why and how the enemy of my soul set that stage for addiction and tried its best to take my life at a very young age. After all, hasn't that been the enemy's strategy — his modus operandi — to endanger, enslave or even to slaughter the next generation?

The Bible, as well as history, reports that evil men of old have throughout the centuries been used as a tool or device of Satan to make assassination attempts, in an attempt to wipe out entire generations of youth, targeting the young males. See, Satan has the understanding and the knowledge that if he can break down, beat up and murder the young men of the upcoming generation, then he cripples and paralyzes mankind overall!

Pharaoh demanded the death of all young males because he wanted to kill all the firstborn, newly born Jewish boys. He saw the Jews were getting bigger, stronger and couples were having a lot of children; therefore Pharaoh started to worry that the Jews would come and take over Egypt. The enemy has always been afraid and tormented that God's people would rise up, take courage, and fulfill their mandate, securing their destiny while turning this world upside down for truth, establishing the Kingdom, abolishing darkness and presenting light to the world in which we live. Pharaoh was not the only ruler that had an assassin's spirit; King Herod demanded the execution of all young male children in the village of Bethlehem, to avoid the loss of his throne to a newborn King, one that many believed to truly be "The King of the Jews."

THE GIFT THAT JUST KEPT ON GIVING

This King was named Jesus, and His birth had been announced and proclaimed. Yes, the enemy of our soul loves it when he can orchestrate a massacre of the innocents, trying to guard against the Kingdom of God being established in our lives.

Not only that, but also through the lives of our offspring and the generations to come!

Pharaoh gave orders to all his people, saying, Every son who comes to birth is to be put into the river...
(Exodus 1:22)

Then the word of Jeremiah the prophet came true, In Ramah there was a sound of weeping and great sorrow, Rachel weeping for her children, and she would not be comforted for their loss.
(Matthew 2:18)

The spirits of Pharaoh and Herod are identical, and are often argued to be synonymous; the spirits of these wicked men are those of destiny destroyers. It is the strongman leading an evil army against the people of God, coming to fight against you and I, in different directions and in various forms of battle, desiring to capture us and bring us into bondage and slavery.

> **The spirit of Pharaoh represents hard slave masters who convert people to captives!**

Everyone's sensitivities in this world have been challenged by the increasingly horrific assaults upon the children and youth of our communities. We see parents themselves who are children, attempting to raise children without the benefit of a successful parenting model. While these situations are tragic and traumatize our psyche, the more brutal assault upon our children and youth is systemic. It has been proven time and time again that the spirit of Pharaoh takes strong measures to bring assault upon the youth of today. *The spirit of Pharaoh makes an assault* **on their minds**, as well as ours; makes an individual believe he or she cannot obtain anything beyond his or her environment.

If a mother is on crack, the child naturally responds and thinks, "I'll be on crack; if Daddy was a drunk and womanizer, then that's what I'll be." We need to realize that there are no limits, nor are there boundaries to where we can go through the power of Christ!

But the people who know their God will display strength and take action.
(Daniel 11:32)

THE GIFT THAT JUST KEPT ON GIVING

I am reminded of a story once told of a baby elephant in the Indian jungle that was separated from his herd and taken into captivity. At the place of captivity, the baby elephant would try to escape, but because the piece of rope tied to his back left leg was too strong for his tender legs, he failed at every attempt. The more he struggled to get away from the piece of rope, the more it tugged and cut at his skin, until one day, the poor baby elephant gave in to the pain and stopped struggling, he stopped in his attempt to move forward. Soon, the piece of rope had become a part of his life — a habit, a second nature, a response. As the baby elephant grew, the piece of rope became comparatively puny. Though the strength of the elephant was now able to break the rope and his freedom attainable, the elephant sat there without a single struggle, because of the simple belief that he could not overcome that piece of rope, what had become a lifestyle to that elephant. The elephant believed mistakenly that he couldn't overcome his environment, all the time having the strength and ability to do so. Similarly with us, as we look at our past, the things that have taken place, all of the major and even minor events that play out so dear to us, everything that we have been through in life, our environment, our circumstances, our defeats, our failures, and the sins in our lives, we then allow these things to paralyze us and keep us from moving forward.

This bond is like the rope that ties us to where we are, and keeps us captive to our sins, environment, and to our past.

I am not sure who you are, where you are from, or what you're going through in this season of your life. But I am sure of one thing: you have the strength to overcome your environment; you do not have to let a piece of rope keep you bound any longer. ***No not for another minute!*** It's time to be set free of every little rope that is holding you back!

Now to him who is able to do in full measure more than all our desires or thoughts, through the power which is working in us.

(Ephesians 3:20)

God's power is already working in you, and His power is greater than any rope that the enemy would try to place on your feet.

His power is greater than the rope of addiction, the rope of abuse, the rope of bitterness, the rope of low self worth and self esteem, the rope of poverty, and all the ropes throughout your life that have tried to hold you down — tried to hold you back from moving forward with God and in God, through God!

This is in fact, your day of Breakthrough!

* The spirit of Pharaoh makes an assault **<u>on their means</u>** — Pharaoh does his best to eliminate opportunities to educate the youth of today, and equip them for financial liberty. This is why we are seeing the greatest amount of high school dropouts, teen pregnancies and overall deprivation in our educational system. But notice what happened when the assassination attempt came against Moses. The Bible tells us that Moses drifted along in a little makeshift ark and was discovered by none other than Pharaoh's daughter!

The offspring of the one trying to assassinate Moses was the one that actually delivered Moses and helped him nurture in strength and wisdom. Moses was later taught and educated very

THE GIFT THAT JUST KEPT ON GIVING

highly. *In other words, your greatest opposition may be who or what God uses to position you in life for greatness.*

  * The spirit of Pharaoh makes an assault **on their manner** — Pharaoh will attack the youth of today concerning lifestyle choices. This spirit was out to capture a young man named Shane West to make him a slave to addiction. I was only fourteen at this time, and it somehow lured me in; this drug seemed so friendly, I had never really felt so good before — it was as if I didn't belong to this world anymore, but had stepped into another.

I felt so free, so alive, so in control, so happy and carefree; in fact, like a small child again. I heard one man later tell of his first time getting high on cocaine. He said it like this, "I felt that I had met my partner for life, no one or nothing would ever wrestle for my affection, for all my affection was lost in this white powder." When I did cocaine for the very first time, I had no idea that it was a setup of the enemy to destroy my life. I had no idea the life — or should I say the hell — that was to be the stage for my teenage years. I did not see it then, but one-quarter gram of cocaine requires and leads to another quarter gram of cocaine. That leads to another gram of cocaine and before you realize it you are in a perpetual direction of a downward fall of addiction; an addiction that leads to a life of misery; an addiction that leads to stealing from family and friends, hurting those that you really love the most.

IT'S TOO LATE, DAD

Yes, my birthday present became my addiction. Soon after, I realized that the one-time escape had now become a lifestyle. I soon found myself no longer "getting high" but using drugs now rather, to merely "get by." I remember one of the saddest moments in my life came the night that my father arrived where I was staying; he later explained to me how he drove for over four hours throughout the city of Fresno, looking for his son, trying his best to find me.

He drove in and out of alleys, looked behind liquor stores and apartments, he drove by areas that were known to be the landing spots of crack heads, and drug users in town, looking for his son. You see by this time Carl West had sobered, and somewhat straightened up his life, gotten remarried and was trying to do what he knew that he should have done twenty years earlier, simply settle down. I was 16 and so very lost in life, he had tried so hard to make a change in his life while I was growing up and I could tell that something had happened for my father, he had been sober now for some time. We sat down together and he began to ask why I was so messed up. He began to ask why we could not make up for lost time. I cried at the table saying, "Dad, you were never there for me and now that you have straightened up your life, mine is so out of control! I am so sorry for who and what I have become."

One of the saddest experiences that I remember with my father was watching him put his face in his hands, crying and saying to me, "I guess my son just doesn't love me anymore." I wanted so bad to scream and yell and by doing so unleash all of the screaming and yelling that I had kept bottled up inside for 16 years! I wanted to scream, **"Dad! I will always love you! I am just bound by this addiction!"**

I couldn't bring myself to say those words, I was at a total loss - all I could do was grind my teeth, keeping my mouth shut, wishing that Shane West could be "fixed or changed" somehow. I just began to wish that things somehow, someway could be

THE GIFT THAT JUST KEPT ON GIVING

different. I really felt that something was dying on the inside of me, but I was so young. I did speak one last time to my dad and I remember saying, "Remember Dad, they all told me I would grow up to be just like you, somehow that happened Dad, somehow that happened!" **And we wept together.**

Periodically, I would visit my aunt and uncle - you remember the ones that lived across from Great America? They moved closer to Fresno, to a small town called Coalinga. There was not much in that town except for a couple restaurants located off of the highway and a Golf Course called Polvadero. My uncle made a purchase of that golf course and promoted the course in hopes of reviving a rather drab community and raise up business interest in the surrounding area. Just them having that golf course caused me to want to visit once again, striking up that fire and love for the game. He allowed me to do some petty work around the golf course, picking up driving range balls, working the register, setting tee times for the golfers, and as time passed I was able to spend a lot of time out there, and in doing so, I found myself constantly sneaking alcohol from the bar.

Of course, nobody knew about this, and so it set a wonderful stage for a young boy that was struggling with addictions, to feed that which I constantly struggled with.

Something happened one night on the property of the golf course, where I stayed quite often, spending the nights at a living quarters area that my uncle had fixed up for guests or employees (I guess at that time I was both). I do desire to go into great detail of what happened at Polvadero, here and now, perhaps at a later time I will be able to discuss this deeper, but I would like to take this opportunity, as I have done publicly in times past, to warn parents to be very careful where you allow your children to stay. Be sure to try to know the homes and the environments that you send your children into. Is it a Christian home where they want to spend the night? Is it a safe place for your child? Are the parents of your child's friend going to be responsible and indeed act as a guardian while your children are in their presence?

I have seen parents that hardly know the parents of their children's friends allow their children to spend nights over at what is simply put "a stranger's house!" Perhaps your child's friend's parents are the greatest in the world but do you know who stops by that home or apartment? What family members may be staying over leading me to once again ask, is it a safe place? Do you know who their family is?

You say, "Shane, you sound paranoid!" No, that is not it at all. I just know from firsthand experience that when a child is left in the trust of others, many times those others are in fact struggling with hang-ups or habits that will have long-reaching effects on the lives of the children that they impose themselves upon.

Even though not aggressively molested, or sexually assaulted in a way that many others have been painfully abused. I was a young man that experienced the inappropriate advances of a man that my family considered to be a friend to the family, and because of this sexual advancement upon me in the morning hours one summer morning, this memory added to the mind games that the enemy of my soul had set me up to play in the coming years of my life.

Let's do all that we can to protect our children, even if it means them becoming mad or angry, thinking that we as parents are too strict.

We have been charged by God to protect their future, have we not?

CHAPTER 7

If This is All That Life Has, Life Sucks

In the early days of my addiction, I would travel to San Francisco where my family member that did cocaine on a daily basis lived. When arriving there, I would know that the lifestyle that I had purposed in my heart to acquire would be there waiting for me.

I was amazed and impressed as a young man, when she and I would stay up for days somehow living that "escaped life." She was a rather influential person. I can recall when staying with her the types of people that would "drop" by for a quick visit only to arrive and leave within five and ten minutes, sometimes not even staying that long.

On one occasion, while looking through her chest of drawers for a straw to use to snort lines, I came across some Police department badges and a bulletproof vest.

When I asked my family member about this, she just simply laughed and said that those items were "job security," giving me the impression that some of her customers were local police officers and detectives, and it was them that would protect her.

It was the summer of 1983 and I was there on the outskirts of San Francisco in Daly City. I made the trip there so that I could attend a huge concert known as *Day on the Green*, being held at the Oakland Coliseum. The lineup was amazing; the concert was featuring *Journey, Triumph, Eddie Money, Bryan Adams,* and *Night Ranger*. This concert was around my birthday in July, and I, along with some friends, was going to go all out on a binge of drinking and "partying."

By this time I had earned a name among the "stoners" and the other druggies at Fresno High School, being a part of the group known as the Veggies. We were planning big times at *Day on the Green*.

While with family and friends, a few men knocked on the door and were invited in. I did not know these guys but I could tell they were probably with the road crew in town for the big concert. As we did cocaine together and as they made their purchase, one of the men asked to see a pair of sunglasses that I was wearing; they were called Vuarnet wraparounds. I loved to wear them due to the leather sides that completely covered and shielded the sun and anyone from seeing bloodshot eyes! I handed the glasses to this guy that we were partying with and he simply said, "Man, these are cool, I have wanted to get me a pair." It was something spoken very casually and I didn't take it too serious, but a few minutes later one of the men that was part of the crew that had walked in a few minutes earlier looked around at a couple of the women that were there (they looked like groupies). This man with rather long black hair and a youthful look said, **"You know, guys, if this is all that life has to offer…then life really sucks!"**

This man named Steve was making the reference to the car that they were driving in, the drugs that they had just purchased and snorted, the expensive trend setting clothes they were wear-

IF THIS IS ALL THAT LIFE HAS, LIFE SUCKS

ing, and the woman that flocked to their side. As he said this we laughed, but once again I did not really take it to heart. A few minutes had passed by and the men decided it was time to get up and get out, so the man that had made a comment about my Vuarnet sunglasses once again put them on and said, "Man, if you let me wear these during the concert, I will get you backstage."

Now make no mistake, I would have loved to have gone backstage to meet these groups, but not at the price tag of my $150.00 pair of Vuarnet "wraparounds," so I respectfully declined his offer asking exactly what part of the road crew was he a part of. The room full of people began to laugh and one of the guys said, "Road crew, that's a good one."

As they left it was told to me who these men were; they were the lead singer, lead guitarist and keyboard player for one of the main bands that were playing the following night! I then was surprised to think about whom it was that had just said, "If this is all that life has to offer, then life sucks."

I wish I would have had some spiritual discernment at that time in my life, and would have really listened to what Steve was saying; those words spoken, if listened to and understood, no doubt would have saved me a lot of trouble!

MORE THAN JUST COCAINE THOUGH

I recently discovered and found that there are over 500,000 recovery groups in our nation at this time. That's right, half a million, but there are only 380,000 churches. So we got more recovery groups than we got churches and there's something wrong with that picture. Within these 500,000 groups — there are at least 20,000,000 (twenty million) people at any given time, who are trying to fix their problem(s) without being educated on the true fixer of the problem(s).

I have never had overly critical or negatives words to say about any group, people, program, meetings, or fellowship that are taking aggressive action to bring sobriety into the lives and into the hearts of men, women and children.

I would just like to present to the world today that the ultimate victory happens when you not only work steps of a program, but you also take steps towards Christ and His atonement that He made at a place called Calvary!

The ultimate answer is not finding a recovery group; the ultimate answer is finding the Recoverer!

I would like to say that addiction does not only seclude itself to drugs and alcohol; there are various forms of addictions. Even the simplest of addictions can be harmful, such as the addiction of gossip. Oh yes, gossip can be addictive can it not? A gossip knows that they're ruining the lives and the friendships of others, but they just can't stop talking.

Over-eaters face addiction, they know they're killing themselves, but they're never satisfied or able to stop binging. Compulsive gamblers know they can't cover their bets but they keep raising the stakes. Over-spenders know the check will bounce but they believe that they have to have what they see. An over-worker knows his family needs him at home but he sacrifices to the career machine. A smoker knows tobacco is destroying his lungs but he needs the next drag. A drinker knows his liver is suffering but he can't stop.

IF THIS IS ALL THAT LIFE HAS, LIFE SUCKS

These are the things that are binding our society. The simple definition of addiction is this - it's when you are powerless to stop something in the face of consequences! Stop and think about what I just said. Addiction is when an individual is powerless to stop something in the face of consequences! Now think, why would a person do that? Don't they know that this is going to happen?

Why would a person go to the gambling boats when they know they're just going to lose all their money?

> ***It's because they're powerless to stop even though they know the consequences.***

It's not that they're ignorant to the consequences; it's that they're powerless to stop themselves despite the consequences. Why would a man continue in an extramarital affair knowing it's a matter of time before he gets caught? Simply because he can't stop himself and this is the power of addiction.

At the time of this book being written, the newspapers, television, internet, as well as all other major media resources, are covering the "breaking news" story of a famous golfer, being caught in what the media is reporting to be over a dozen extramarital affairs.

This man that has been noted to be worth a billion dollars, having a beautiful wife, and children at home, not to mention multi-million dollar business endorsements, somehow decided to jeopardize it all, for what appeared to be a "good time" with women, ranging from strippers to super models. It's not that people are not aware of the consequences and haven't tasted the consequences; it's just that within themselves they lack the power and the strength to overcome that which they're addicted to. Alcoholism and drug addiction, including addiction to prescription drugs, is running rampant and ruining the countless lives of Americans today.

Statistics say that one out of every fourteen people in our nation is addicted to alcohol, and one out of every twenty people has an ongoing addiction to drugs.

Drugs are not all that is wrecking havoc in our homes though; work-holism is seen in long hours extended at work, weekly business trips, many hours working at home and even during vacation. This is more of an acceptable form of addiction; we just say that person is a hard worker but what about his or her work preoccupation? Never can disengage, never can socialize, and never can spend quality time with family including his or her children that need that parent's relationship more than just a handful of hellos and goodbyes through every month.

People trying to climb the corporate ladder and addicted to success.

Did you know you could be addicted to success?

There are people who are addicted to climbing the ladder of success so much so they ruin their family and they go through marriage after marriage, destroying the lives of their children all in the name of making a few more dollars every year and having a better office view, a bigger condo, or the ability to drive that special icon vehicle of success.

Sex addictions, including internet pornography, cyber relationships, pedophilia, and prostitution— there are so many souls hurting in our country addicted to sexual addictions and they cannot stop. Some people are bound to media addictions.

I don't know if you've seen on the internet there's a You Tube video of a young man whose mother erases his *War of Worlds* account, a fantasy world that you can live in on the computer. When this young man came home and found out that his mother had erased his account and his countless hours of fantasy world were gone, he began to manifest hatred and rage; he began to bang his head into the walls, punching walls and even himself with a shoe, screaming and ripping his clothes off, as if he were demon possessed, running around, in and out of his closet, all the time his rage being secretly caught on video tape. Why?

Because this generation of people are losing themselves in a Cyber World of Fantasy!

There are so many forms of addiction — eating disorders, anorexia, bulimia, overeating, the use of food as a means of controlling emotions and the hoarding of food.

Over 4,000,000 Americans are hopelessly lost in eating disorders and food addictions to where the person somehow medicates themselves though food consumption. They are addicted, as well as any and all other people that would somehow fit into one category or another, from the above-mentioned addictions and compulsive behaviors, but let me please continue and simply saying; **Shane West needed to be rescued by the power of the cross!**

CHAPTER 8

The Discovery of Crack Cocaine

By the time I was approaching sixteen, my nasal passage and the ability for me to inhale the powder cocaine had far left me because of my harsh addiction and daily drug abuse. Now this teenager saw himself with constant nosebleeds and dropping out of school, stealing often to get high, and it was during this time that my so called friends from the West Side came to Shane West with a brand new revelation. They said, "There is no longer a need to try to continue to inhale or snort cocaine, there is an even easier way, a more 'high' way to get high, and escape. Shane, just do what others are doing over here on the West Side — 'rock it up.'"

"You don't have to snort or inhale powder, there's a simple process where you can just take the powder, and turn it into rock cocaine to smoke, get a better high, a bigger rush, a greater intensity. Shane this stuff will *"ring your bells."*

So there, just in my early years, not even sixteen years of age as of yet, was the first time that I was introduced to crack cocaine. Long before crack cocaine was called crack cocaine, we just called it rock up. Long before Richard Pryor caught himself on fire doing it, I began doing it! We would take the powder substance we bought off the streets or from our fixes and our friends and we would mix that with baking soda to produce a purified form of cocaine. Then we would put it on a pipe. (Sometimes the pipe was something that was purchased from a paraphernalia store, or many times a broken rusty antenna off an old vehicle, with a Brillo pad or something that could be used as a screen.) **With that, we began to freebase cocaine.**

It is true what they say about crack: when you take that first hit, that high that a person gets for the first time, he or she will run and chase after for the rest of their lives, never catching it again, but simply bound to a chase, where there is no finish line.

I chased after it, but I could never find it. In that chase I hurt those all around me and lost everything in my life… well almost everything, I still had my soul, but my soul seemed like trash! Many nights were spent in the alleys. Yes, many cold nights were spent in project and apartment complexes with boarded-up windows and red tags from the city of Fresno. These places were condemned places that I would live and spend nights just looking for a high. Looking for an answer to a question that I was not so sure of; searching for something that I didn't really know that I was searching for.

By the time I was sixteen years of age, I was a crack head. This boy that many thought would be so popular was now living on the streets, because I would steal from family and friends, I would lie and cheat, I would do anything and everything, chasing that high.

THE DISCOVERY OF CRACK COCAINE

ANGELS IN THE ALLEY

I can remember many nights, because of the coldness of the winters in Fresno, sleeping in such strange places. My family, having washed their hands of me, friends (if you could call them that), knowing that I was a crack addict, stopped speaking to me, and so I did not have many places to go. **I would go on binges, drug binges, and I would steal for the drug.**

I would try to hustle for the rock or the crack cocaine and many nights I remember going in the back alleys off of Shields Avenue, and I can still remember and sense the feelings of loneliness, despair, and abandonment that would rush over me as I would walk the streets, the back alleys. I would go in the alleys of apartment complexes, into the laundry rooms, hoping that people had washed and dried their clothes in the washrooms and that the clothes dryers would still be warm enough that I could cuddle against them to find warmth in the early morning hours while ice was still on the ground! In the morning, I would think…"My God help me. It's four, five, six, seven a.m. and the sun is coming up and I have wasted yet another day. Another night of despair has passed, what in the world has become of Shane West?"

Still tripping on this crack cocaine, but it was so cold. **IT WAS SO VERY LONELY!**

Many times I would huddle my back against the wall and I would shake and I would shiver and wonder, "Is my life ever going to get better? Am I ever going to be set free?" Sixteen years of age and there I began to wrestle with manic depression, even thoughts of ending it all, taking my life, yes thoughts of suicide.

A dear friend of mine named Ronnie did that very thing, one weekend. Ronnie was a very handsome, charismatic young man that by all appearances had the world by the tail. Ronnie seemed to have life really moving forward for him. I remember him pulling up in his blue corvette and as he climbed out of that car looking like something coming out of a stage production or movie set in Hollywood. I said, "Ronnie, looks like you're winning!"

Ronnie laughed and answered back to me saying, "SK, I'm going to win even if I lose." His answer caught me off guard, and was quite puzzling to me. I remember thinking, man that was awkward; but you see I did not know at the time what exactly was on his mind. I did know that Ronnie had stopped by looking for my brother and my brother was not there so Ronnie quickly left. Ronnie went on a killing rampage in Fresno a few minutes later. It was later discovered that the reason for him stopping by asking me about others like my brother Steve, and another man named Al, was that he had them on his list of those that he had committed and vowed to "take out with him." We all had suspected Ronnie's involvement in drugs but could never get that verified by anyone. Ronnie married and had a son that often was seen traveling with Ronnie in his corvette, driving sidekick down Blackstone Avenue, the two of them were a sight to see. Ronnie had made a purchase of cocaine and unbeknownst to him the cocaine had been tainted, the powder had been poisoned; it had been laced with battery acid, by a man that was having an affair with his wife, and once Ronnie began inhaling that poisoned powder it immediately began to eat and attack his central nerve system. Soon after he was poisoned, Ronnie began losing his ability to walk and function as that battery acid had an irreversible effect on his nerves.

THE DISCOVERY OF CRACK COCAINE

Ronnie pledged to kill as many people and to take as many down with him in his death (including police officers) as was possible, some of the friends of my brother, if not my brother as well. Hours later, the reports began to circulate through the streets and then on the news, every local channel reporting that there was a gunman at large killing people.

First, Ronnie made contact at a bar, where he knew the bartender, the same man that was having an affair with his wife. The bartender did not know that Ronnie knew all the details about the affair and the tainted drugs, and so when Ronnie invited him outside to do a few lines of cocaine with his old friend, the bartender followed behind but as he got seated into Ronnie's vehicle, the bartender was met with a gun barrel to his face and Ronnie pulled the trigger. He then went looking for his wife and other men in our city. When it was all said and done, many lives were taken that night. Late that night Ronnie was on the phone with the local authorities, news, and family, barricaded in a house, they found him shut in, after the police surrounded him…he said, "This is where Ronnie says goodbye." Ronnie pulled the trigger while still speaking on the telephone with a loved one, and just like that Ronnie was gone. Diving headfirst into an eternity, like a diver diving in the black of night into a bottomless pool, leaving his young son behind and the memories of a man that many people, including myself thought was "winning."

But you see when you are concerned with only winning in life through possessions; you often lose the things that matter most!

Crack cocaine does take a person higher than what powder cocaine can offer, but with a greater high came the greater depression; with a greater rush came the greater oppression, and the paranoia would set in, and I would feel that I too, like Ronnie would be better off dead. I would shake and tremble and I would wonder to myself - what is my life going to become?

I felt like a bum, a loser, a runaway train headed for destruction that could not be stopped!

Why was I born? Why did I not have a normal childhood? Why didn't my father love me enough to stay with me? My mind would rush back to when I was seven or eight years old and I would see my mother's face as she would point her finger in my face and my direction and say, "Shane, you're going to be a bum. You're going to be an alcoholic." I would remember that and I would put my head in my hands in that laundry room and cry uncontrollably.

I could remember as if it were but just yesterday and I would weep and I would sob and I'd ask myself, I would speak and often scream out, "Is my life really going to wind up like my father's? Am I a bum? Am I an alcoholic and addict? Have I, in fact, turned into the image of my father, after swearing that I would never be like him? Is this what I was born to be? Is this my destiny? This must be a nightmare! I know that any minute now I am going to awake and be a young child again, playing with my family…awake to be sitting at a dinner table with my mother and father like a normal family. I know that any second I am going to wake and be at a park happily sliding down a slide into my father's arms…this has to be a bad dream!"

I was 16 years old and now frequently visiting Alcoholics Anonymous and Narcotics Anonymous meetings looking for a way out of this hell. I remember what it was like to introduce myself at the age of 16, "Hi, my name is Shane. I'm an alcoholic," or, "Hi, my name is Shane, I'm an alcoholic/addict."

But I was always looking for something.
I was always looking for a way out!

THE DISCOVERY OF CRACK COCAINE

I tried counseling. I tried different Detox Centers, but everywhere that I looked and it seemed everywhere that I turned, I could not find what I needed to overcome this cocaine addiction and this alcoholism that was running rampant in my life.

Trash was all that my life was, and trash was what I figured my life would always be.

CHAPTER 9

Memorial Day, 1984

Looking back now I can count and reflect the many times I could have truly lost my life. I had a girlfriend who at that time, like many teenagers, I just knew that she would be the girl that I would marry. Her parents owned a cabin at Shaver Lake, not too far of a drive from Fresno and Shaver Lake, and the mountain areas were always a scenic getaway for both the young and the old. I recall driving up to Shaver Lake with friends while doing drugs and boozing.

We thought it would be a great idea to break into a cabin and kick it watching some sports, and playing some "quarters." For those that may not know what "quarters" is, it's a game of tossing a "quarter" off a tabletop on one bounce, landing it off the bounce into a small "shot size" glass or cup. If you sank your quarter, your opponent had to drink a shot of whiskey or beer and the object of the game was to get your opponent wasted, a game that I always bragged of being the champion of. So we broke into a vacant cabin, (not the one that my girlfriend's parents owned; they had already accused me of scratching or "keying" their vehicle so please let me set the record straight. This was not a cabin owned by my girlfriend's family, neither was it a cabin of anyone that we knew for that matter, and all that we were wanting was a place to spend some time and get wasted), and after doing so we headed back to Fresno. While drunk and intoxicated, trying to drive and navigate the sharp turns that led from the Shaver area, back down into the valley, I began scaring my friends Andy, Mark and Paul…they began to ask me to pull over and get some fresh air. They said, "You're too wasted to be driving man, SK you're driving crazy."

So I thought, "If you want to see crazy - watch this!" I began to accelerate to a high speed and within a moment I approached a sharp curve that I could not make at that rate of speed, slamming on the brakes while turning the steering wheel as hard as I could only to begin to skid out of control, rotating in circles, unable to gain control of my car. By the time our vehicle stopped skidding in circles and came to rest, we quickly looked over to the driver's side and saw how close to death we had actually come. When I opened my driver's side door and immediately looked down I saw the edge of a mountain so close to that edge I remember thinking to myself, "I do not even have enough land area or dirt area to place my foot upon to get out of this car on the driver's side." We were literally at the edge of a cliff looking over!

If it had not been for the Grace of God that day my vehicle would have swept off the mountain and my life would have been swept into eternity high on cocaine and drunk on Old English 800 Malt Liquor Beer.

But this was not the only time that I was spared, I could take you to the condemned apartments where many times taking a hit off of a freebase pipe I would vomit, vomit up blood and feel that my chest was going to explode, many times after being up for days on cocaine, my heart beating so fast that I just knew that I was going to stroke out right then and there, many times

MEMORIAL DAY, 1984

looking at a pistol, hearing the words "Kill yourself Shane, it's really the only way out – kill yourself and let that trash burn for all eternity!"

At the age of 18, just prior to my high school graduation, I was involved in a car accident that took the life of an individual. Thankfully, it was an early enough hour on the Tuesday after Memorial Day 1984, and I had not taken a drink of alcohol nor done any drugs that day. I was driving the vehicle and carrying my friends Paul and Jeff, when in the intersection two vehicles collided and there in that intersection I watched as a man got out of his pickup truck, walked a few steps and fell over dead. A few days later the Class of 1984 – Fresno High School graduated, I was alone in a hospital bed.

It was later revealed that the driver of that pick-up truck was high on marijuana, and even though the tests proved that I was not driving under the influence, and the accident was not my fault, I was still part of a tragedy that cost a man his life, and the trauma that I experienced through that car accident was horrific.

The district attorney's office investigated the vehicle homicide and considered pressing charges, largely in part, I believe, because of my reputation concerning drugs in the city that I lived in. Even though Fresno is rather a large city, in the early 80's I still remember it having a hometown mentality, and it seemed that everyone knew something about someone!

My father had a long-time drinking buddy named William A. Smith - he was the former district attorney in Fresno. My father asked if he could help his son Shane and Mr. Smith agreed to, therefore, there were never any formal charges or legal issues other than insurance companies fighting over payoffs and civil suit claims.

William A. Smith was a man that gave great help to my father and I, ironically, he was also the same man that was hired ten years later by the man that murdered my father. Just as Mr. Smith no doubt used his former D.A. influence on my behalf, that same influence got a man acquitted of murdering my father, but that's another book, isn't it?

At 19 years of age, it seemed as though my life was even growing darker into depression and oppression. Suicidal thoughts had been running through my mind for many, many years and I remember putting a pistol to my head and wondering, "Who would really care if I ended my life?"

But whatever it was, now that I look back, I must say that it was the mercy of God that kept me from pulling the trigger at the age of 19. I staggered in a dark world and I felt all alone, and somebody reading this book right now might feel that you're all alone, but Shane West has penned these words to tell you that you are in fact not alone.

The presence of God is watching over you, just as His presence, love and grace watched over me through robberies, thefts, and car accidents, drug binges, and homelessness, helplessness at a young age, and nights that I would vomit after taking a massive hit off a cocaine pipe — while my heart would pound through my chest, people laughing as they watched my heart beat through the shirt that I was wearing. **A freebase pipe had become everything to me!**

It had become my girlfriend, my family, my best friend, and it was my world! It seemed as though my life had gotten to a place that I was probably trying to kill myself, but the Grace of God would not let me go.

CHAPTER 10

From Bad to Worse

From the age of 14 until I was 21, I was a cocaine addict and I was an alcoholic, constantly looking and needing drugs to sustain my life. I know what it's like to get down on my hands and knees and go through the shag rugs of apartments in condemned apartment complexes and projects and go through the back seats of automobiles just looking for some little kibbles and bits to throw back up on a freebase pipe. Looking through shag rugs and throwing breadcrumbs up on the pipe and throwing soap up on the pipe just always tripping, always looking for some more drugs to find a high, because no matter how many drugs I did, it never would bring peace. I know what it's like watching mothers prostitute themselves in bathrooms while their children are left in the kitchen eating cold chicken noodle soup out of a can, no electricity in the shabby apartment because Momma has spent all of her welfare check and all of her money on crack cocaine, failing to pay the utilities bill.

One cold winter night I took a trip to the west side of the city to find a place that I could take the powder cocaine that I had obtained and "rock it up," turning it into a freebase form of cocaine. I had a buddy of mine named Joe riding with me, directing me to the right apartment complex so that we could make this happen. Joe knew that I had somewhat of a substantial amount of powder in my possession, enough to keep us high and smoking the pipe for at least a couple of days. We arrived at a certain apartment and Joe told me to stay in the car while he ran into the apartment and made sure that we would be able to use the kitchen and the apartment for a while. Joe had gone into the apartment and did not come out for awhile; something felt wrong but I just attributed it to "tripping" and "tweaking" from the drugs that we had already done together before taking the drive over to the west side. Before I knew what was happening, several men came and surrounded my car demanding that I get out, one of the men took a knife and placed it to my throat while the other men screamed at him, "Cut him! Cut him, man!" Quickly, the man that held the knife to my neck and I made eye contact; that eye contact probably helped save my life that night because I knew who this guy was.

My brother Steve owned a gym in Fresno where a lot of the body builders, power lifters and Fresno State football players all worked out. This young man yielding the knife that night was in fact a young man that came into my brother's gym often, and played for Fresno State and I knew who he was; likewise he looked surprised to find out who it was that he was on the verge of killing. He had a reputation in Fresno because of his influence as a gym owner - knowing all the "right" people, having "connections" he himself being a big power lifter not to mention the cops as well as the thugs that came into the gym on a daily basis; therefore, I believe that this young black man knew that he had already gone too far by robbing me, but slicing my throat was something that he did not want to do and have my brother find out.

The young man slightly took the knife away from my throat and screamed at me to run, "Get outta here man, run for your

FROM BAD TO WORSE

life!" and that is exactly what I did. I ran and I ran until I got out of that particular section of the west side known simply as the "drive-thru" (because of the fact that anyone, at any time, could simply drive through that area and make purchases of drugs and narcotics of any kind).

I ran to a pay phone where I called 911 reporting that I had been car jacked and needed help. When the Fresno Police Department rolled up, they waited for several units to arrive before proceeding to the "drive-thru" area of apartments, and while an officer took the report he said to me, "Son, I do not know who you are, or where you are from, nor do I know what you were really doing over here, being the only white boy within twelve city blocks, but somebody was looking out for you tonight, and you better thank God for it."

How true that was. Can you think back to the times that we traveled beyond a safe place not only geographically but also spiritually, and if it had not been for the Lord that saved us?

When that young man held the knife to my throat, I firmly believe that there was an angel that was quickly dispatched that kept that boy from doing me any harm. Why? Simply because God had plans for me, God had chosen to use me from the foundation of the worlds; while I was yet in the womb of my mother, God had called me, God had chosen me, and God knew that as much as hell wanted it to happen, I could not die there that cold foggy night. God had a turnaround for me in my future.

Today is December 31, 2009. As I am writing I hear my three sons speak with excitement about New Year's Eve. My mind travels back to New Year's Eve 1986, where I remember being huddled up against a wall in an alley, as the time was being counted down for the New Year to be ushered in!

The sounds of laughter and firecrackers could be heard, the sights of fireworks could be seen from this little alley where I was.

People were celebrating closing out the old year, bringing in the new. Shane West had nothing to celebrate, nothing to look forward to in the coming year. I had no idea that the coming year would be the year of turnaround for my life!

> *Before you were formed in the body of your mother I had knowledge of you, and before your birth I made you holy; I have given you the work of being a prophet to the nations.*
> (Jeremiah 1:5)

I was told by Mother many times that I was a mistake…was I? I think not.

CHAPTER 11

November 5 – Recycled by Grace

Early in the morning on November 5, 1987, I decided enough was enough.

This was going to be the last day I was tormented by this demon called cocaine! This was going to be the last time I went through an addicted day and night. No more reflections on what should have been in my life, or what could have been in my childhood. I grabbed a pistol that was nearby, a stolen pistol, as a matter of fact, and put it up to my head. I had thought about suicide many times in the past, but this time it was very different.

This time I had confidence that I was, in fact, going to pull the trigger. Contrary to past times, I no longer cared or worried about what my parents would say around my casket. I was no longer concerned with their tears; after all, were they ever really concerned with mine? I thought, "This is the day that Shane West dies."

I could see myself reading my obituary — *a 21 year old crack head commits suicide in Fresno, California.*

I put the pistol to my temple and squeezed, squeezing as hard as I could – just like the enemy that had slowly squeezed the life, happiness and joy out of this young boy, who was now a man, a loser with no direction in life. I held the pistol tightly and squeezed again, but something came over me — something said, "Don't do this!"

Something came over me and said, ***"It's not over yet!"***

I put the pistol down on the makeshift bed next to me, knelt down and began weeping. I sobbed uncontrollably, but in a different way than ever before. I felt so much sorrow in my heart. I knew I was going to pull the trigger. The thought visited my mind again, "This is the night that Shane West dies." I felt the sorrow of knowing I had wasted my entire life! I felt the sorrow of knowing my life had been wasted in addictions, wasted on the streets, and hurting everyone that was around me.

Something very powerful happened to me at this time, I suddenly realized, and could actually see and understand, just how much my life had been spent **"shackled"** in the prison house of addiction. I saw how I had hurt others so very much. I had the attitude that if you couldn't do anything for me, or you couldn't give me something that would help and enable me to get high, then you were nothing to me. But, if I saw a chance to get something from you - look out! I would con you, steal from you, cheat you, hurt you, or do whatever it took to get what I wanted, more cocaine. Your feelings didn't matter to me at all. Nothing mattered except me, and cocaine. Wow! This was really the first time that this had dawned on me in such a realistic way.

When I was at the end of my rope, there I found hope.

I knew that nothing outside of Christ was going to bring me genuine comfort, peace, acceptance, love and forgiveness - things I had sought all my life, just not knowing where to really look. As I look back I see where I allowed the enemy to influence my

NOVEMBER 5 — RECYCLED BY GRACE

life with fear, shame and condemnation, especially regarding my many failures at trying to break free from my addictions. Even though I thought for sure my life was over, God had other plans!

As I knelt down beside the bed early that morning, I did not understand that what was happening on the outside was actually a mirror reflection, or expression, of my soul to God that was taking place on the inside…total surrender! I had never been to church. I had never gone to Sunday school. Nobody had ever knocked on my door and told me about the love of God.

Nobody had ever come up to me at Fresno High School and said, "Shane West, your life is a mess but Jesus Christ loves you just as you are."

I had never picked up or read a Bible, or even a truck stop track, for that matter.

I knew nothing about God. Yet, something spoke to me, "Don't pull the trigger." Something said, "Why don't you try something different?"

"Why don't you try to cry out to God?"

As I knelt on my knees in that little converted garage, against the little makeshift bed, I began to pray. I cried out to a God that I had never known; a God I had never been introduced to. I simply said, "God, if you're out there, if you're real, if there really is a God, there must be a reason I made it all these years; the drugs didn't kill me, the alcohol didn't kill me, the streets did not kill me, even a switchblade knife couldn't take my life. There has to be a reason for my existence. There just has to be!" I wept and pleaded,

> *"God, if you're out there, I want you to make yourself known to me."*

Then, in the early morning hours of November 5, 1987, the presence of God Almighty moved in that little converted garage in Fresno, California. It was as if a hundred pounds was lifted from my shoulders — a great weight of sin taken away from my soul.

And God spoke to me, *"Son, I have given you a life and that life has been wasted, now pick yourself up and follow me. If you follow me, I promise I will show you the peace and love that you have searched for all of these years."*

I stood up and threw my hands into the air and said, "God, I don't even know who you are, but I believe that you spoke to me. I heard your voice speak to my heart and I have decided to follow you." (Looking back now, I believe that standing and raising my hands was my natural way of furthering my surrender.) I knew that something miraculous had taken place. I had truly just found that "high" I had been looking for all my life but it did not come by way of a substance or through a pipe. The peace and joy, the happiness, and feeling of being loved that I had been desperately searching for, guess what? I had just found it! I found it through the grace of God.

I was totally shocked how my life could have been transformed the way that it was transformed. Immediately the desire for drugs and alcohol left!

Immediately the desire to do others wrong left. Immediately the way that I began to talk changed. The words that came from my mouth immediately were softening. My heart and mind had been touched by God!

NOVEMBER 5 — RECYCLED BY GRACE

> *...and the valiant men whose hearts God had touched...*
> (1 Samuel 10:26)

I had just found the power of Grace!

FINDING TREASURE UNDER THE TRASH

Something that I have often noticed in the faith based community is we say, *"That's the day I found God."* When making references to the day of our spiritual awakening, we say that we found *"Him"* when in all actuality *"He"* was never lost. Would it not be more truthful and accurate when we share our testimony with others, to say *"God found us"* when we were the ones that were really lost!?

    I remember a woman who had mistakenly dropped her very expensive wedding ring into a small trash can located near her kitchen sink. She discovered this mishap but it was too late, because the trash collectors had already came and removed the trash bags to take to the city dump. She was not only crushed because of the monetary value of the ring, but she knew that this wedding band had been handed down for several generations. To her it was priceless! The woman who had been married for 55 years was devastated in her loss. Her husband Angelo promised her that he would do everything possible to get that ring back.

So the couple contacted the trash processing center and requested help in the search to find this wedding ring of great value. The workers that day explained to Angelo that there was over 20 tons of trash, and they could not possibly think they would find this "needle in a haystack," but Angelo's persistence, and his wife's broken heart and countenance, led the workers to agree in helping search and sift through the garbage. Many hours were spent that day searching for this lost treasure. The searching paid off! Nine hours after a relentless search through the garbage of that city, pile after pile, hundreds of trash bags being open and searched though, they finally found it, the treasure that was in the trash!

The story made local news and Angelo said, "We went through trash for several hours, but we spotted it, we pulled it out, how we found that ring, I really don't know." Then Angelo said, "It's amazing how this occurred, miracles still happen!" Without washing it and without cleaning it off, Angelo quickly found his wife and slipped the ring back on her finger, only before making her promise that she would never lose it again.

I am not sure if you know where I am going with this story, but I would like to say that we, as God's creation, were tossed into the trash bin. It does not matter what your last name is, what city or town that you were born in or who your parents are or are not. We were all discarded, and considered trash by the enemy of our soul, but I am so glad today that *"What is one man's trash is another man's treasure!"* Through the many tons of trash and debris in our lives, there was One that went looking for us. He has been searching for us for a really long time. I know that we often have the mindset that we are all alone, and God does not even know our name, but please be assured that He knows exactly where we are today. You may be in some junk or your life may appear to be at the county dump, your ways may be trashy, but remember, *"What is one man's trash is another man's treasure!"*

NOVEMBER 5 — RECYCLED BY GRACE

Everyone that knew Shane West said that he was a loser, a junkie, a crack head. Just a back alley, gutter living, homeless, drug addict that would do anything for his next fix, or hit of crack cocaine.

Jesus came looking through the trash though! He didn't mind getting His hands dirty searching for me. Jesus knew that even though there were tons of trash, hurts and hang-ups, issues that were unresolved, and an overall trashy life, somewhere beneath all of that, there was a treasure that He just had to continue searching for! Jesus found that **"treasure in the trash"** the night of November 5, 1987 and I have never been the same! He decided to clean me up, remove the staunch and decay of sin that was in my life and use me for His Purpose!

I WILL NEVER BE THE SAME AGAIN

Soon after, I went into the house to search for a Bible.

Something was telling me to pick up a Bible. I found a Bible and wiped away the age-old dust from its leather cover. I quickly opened it to a scripture that read, "Go ye therefore and teach all nations baptizing them in the name of the Father, the Son, and Holy Ghost." I said, "Lord Jesus, it sounds like you're putting a calling on my life."

"It sounds like there's been a reason that I have survived these twenty-one years. It sounds as though there is something you've got planned for me." At that time, at that moment of my Christian experience, I knew not the scripture…

> *But when God, who had set me apart even from my mother's womb, and called me through His Grace, was pleased to reveal His Son in me so that I might preach Him.*
> (Galatians 1:15-16)

I remember that I turned to Matthew 28:19 and it shocked me. It was almost as if the Word was becoming flesh and ministering to me face-to-face. The presence of the Lord touched me in such a way that I was almost "in shock." I quickly shut that Bible, being dismayed, and quite honestly a bit afraid. I spoke to the Lord saying, "Lord Jesus, if this is you speaking to me, let me open this Bible to the very same verse again! I have only opened it once before, but I want to open it again and I want you to speak to me again, if this is really you."

Lo and behold, I opened that Bible to the very same scripture,

"Go ye therefore and teach all nations baptizing them in the name of the Father, the Son, and the Holy Ghost."

I closed the Bible the second time and asked, "Lord God, if I can do it one more time, just one more time, then I know I will have a calling on my life to do something for you." I closed my eyes and flipped that Bible around in circles a few times in my hands, and once again opened the scripture – there it was the third time!

"Go ye therefore and teach all nations baptizing them in the name of the Father, the Son, and the Holy Ghost."

NOVEMBER 5 — RECYCLED BY GRACE

Guess what? This boy, Shane West, the crack addict, Fresno's biggest loser, who many people gave up on, the one that was told all of his life that he was a loser - I finally felt like a winner! I felt that I had purpose in my life. I knew that God was real, and that He wanted to use me for a Divine purpose!

I had just went from Cocaine to the Calling –
Recycled By Grace!

re·cy·cle
1: to pass again through a series of changes or treatments
2: to return or to bring again to an original condition so that operation can begin
3: to reclaim for future use

Anyone who belongs to Christ has become a new person. The old life is gone; a new life has begun!
(2 Corinthians 5:17)

Through the many years now of my sobriety, I have had opportunities to reflect upon the sickness of addictions, both in my life and the lives to whom I have ministered to. Whether the addiction is to drugs, alcohol, sex, or anything else for that matter, each addiction can be addressed and summarized into five steps.

The first step that I fell prey to was that **I was unprepared.**

I really didn't know what to expect or what was to follow. I began to taste of something that I had never tasted of before, and while thinking this was to be just a "high" here and there, it instead became a horrible lifestyle. I was unprepared to deal with the feeling that drugs and alcohol gave me. Now I have heard many ministers and adults attempt to say that sin is not fun, drugs don't make you feel good, but that's not actually a true statement. There is temporary fun in sin according to our Bibles.

Sure sin and addiction may be fun at first, but the payday that comes afterward is heartbreaking.

> *Moses believed that it was better to undergo pain with the people of God, rather than to enjoy the pleasures of sin for a season.*
> *(Hebrews 11:25)*

Sin may have pleasures but the end results are death, I was unprepared and uneducated in this area.

The second step is something that I refer to as **friendship**. What is friendship? Friendship is where I began choosing friends involved in the addiction. I began to change the nature of my relationships. I began to hang out with people who made me feel comfortable with the direction that I was heading. I have emphasized greatly through the years that our children need Christian fellowship! Our churches need a youth group, parents, and leaders that will demonstrate unconditional love and acceptance to our children. Does this mean that we advocate sin and transgressions? Absolutely not, but if and when our children fall, fail and come up short, we do not need to chase them away but rather embrace them showing our youth firsthand the love of Jesus Christ. We do not love them on the condition that they merit our love; we love them unconditionally, as Christ loved us!

The third stage is **infatuation and denial**. One begins to blame others for the trouble, the actions and the addictions that are controlling their lives. In this stage, infatuation is where the first consequences begin to happen but yet it's completely ignored because the hold that addiction has on the mind and spirit. I became so infatuated with cocaine that the infatuation that I had for the drug would override the horrible repercussions that the drug brought to my life and family. They get that first DUI and they just blow right through it. Instead of being horrified at the direction that I was going,

I would pass right through the warning signs, without ever missing an opportunity to get "High."

Next, comes **love and betrayal** where an addiction becomes life controlling; a daily involvement. The entire family now revolves around the addiction. Everyone around me was forced to both recognize and yield to what was happening, or they were pushed far out of your life. I would have the mindset, I will love you as long as you accept what I am and what I am doing, but if you don't accept what I'm into then it's over between us!

How many times have parents felt guilty for drawing a line in the sand with their kids and their kids putting them out of their life? Love and betrayal causes the addict to choose their addiction over those who love them, and those who would have their best interest at heart.

Fifth and finally we ascend to the **place of worship**. This is where our addiction becomes the highest priority in life, above all other relationships and interests. Total enslavement to the power or should I say powerlessness over our addiction(s) a demonic power. All that matters is worship to the drug of choice or the addicts binge. I would walk great distances for cocaine. I would steal for cocaine. I would lie for cocaine. I would worship cocaine without really understanding what exactly I was doing! Jesus Christ came to set us free of the five steps of addiction. If you are struggling with an addiction, let's take a step towards Christ right now and please allow me to pray with you this simple prayer. If you pray also having a mind made up to be set free you will be set free!

> *If therefore the Son shall make you free,*
> *ye shall be free indeed.*
> (John 8:36)

LET'S PRAY TOGETHER

I would like to pray with you right now, just you and I as you read this book,

"Lord Jesus, I look to you as my refuge today, a very present help in time of trouble. Jesus you are my fortress, and strength! I confess that I am guilty of sin, iniquity, and transgression. I submit to you, God. I draw near to you that you may draw near to me. I pray in Jesus Name that you cleanse my hands and purify my heart. Take this life of mine and remove it from the powers that hold me back."

NOVEMBER 5 — RECYCLED BY GRACE

"I humble myself in the presence of the Lord that He may exalt me, and find the treasure that is in the trash. I repent of my sins."

"The Word is near me, in my mouth and in my heart. I confess with my mouth that Jesus Christ is Lord and believe in my heart that God raised Him from the dead. Forgive me now, and cleanse me through the work of Calvary."

"Today I ask you to completely cleanse me, my body, mind, will, and emotions. Deliver me Lord, from this day forward. In Jesus' name I pray. Amen."

I am so grateful that God saved and delivered me right out of my addiction and sin. I am thankful, too, that I had my spiritual awakening in that little converted garage and not in a beautiful church building full of religious people that would not understand that grace could in fact reach a wretch like Shane West. A church with members who perhaps would have looked down upon me because of my tattered clothes or the smell of my unbathed body, sweating so much while "sweating" a freebase pipe so often!

If I had visited a church, would I have heard about the unconditional love and mercy of Jesus Christ? Or, would I have perhaps heard the dos and don'ts of religion? Would I had been told and instructed on how to "*merit*" the love of God?

I was not *forced* to get my life together, or straighten up and get sober **before** coming to God. I was assured by His Grace that He loved me. He loved me **before** I had my act together. He saw not where I was, but where I could be, where I could go, who I could reach, the people I could help — that's what God saw November 5, 1987!

Many people fail to understand this experience – this "God thing" is not about a set of beliefs or theories. Theories won't get the trash out of your heart and out of your life. Let me take you back just before Christ was born some 2,000 plus years ago.

Remember the story of Christ's birth, Joseph and Mary? I know that most of us can recall the story, even if by memory of the Christmas Story. The Angel of the Lord told Joseph about what had happened to Mary and the plans for the future. The Angel said, "She will give birth to a son and you are to give him the name Jesus, which means he always saves, because he will save his people from their sins." ***Jesus saves us from our sins. He saves us from our trashed lives.***

I remember once in an alley looking for a high, seeing an old rugged man walking down the alley with a shopping cart. As he walked, he shouted, almost singing, "Trash man…here comes the trash man." He was saying, "Set your trash out, I will collect all the unwanted trash."

That sounds like Jesus, does it not? While still in my junk, living a trashy life, in a stinky environment, Jesus came walking down the alley of my life saying, "The trash man is coming. Lay all your cares upon me, for I do care for you. Give me your trash, I will exchange it for a testimony; give me your mess, I will recycle that mess and give you a message. Give me your pain and I will give you healing; give me your debts, I will deliver you. I want you to give me your fears, because I have plenty of favor to bestow upon you! Give me your past, I have your future; give me your death, I have life for you, more than that, the life that I give is the *"abundant life."* Give me your failures, to me failures are not fatal, nor are they final!

I am Jesus Christ, aka The Trash Man, I can take what looks to be a trashed life and RECYCLE IT for my own use!"

NOVEMBER 5 — RECYCLED BY GRACE

Remember the prayer that is often referred to as the "Serenity Prayer," found in Mathew 6:10 – the Lord prayed and gave us instruction to have this prayer radiate from our hearts, "Your will be done in earth as it is in Heaven." Many people quote that incorrectly, saying "<u>on</u> earth as it is in Heaven" – but if one does not read it clearly, one misses the impact of that prayer; we must pray that His will be done "***in earth***." I am reminded that we as people were formed from what? *The dust of the earth!*

We were made by dust, by sand, by soil, if you please; therefore, Christ gave us this example. Please read it again, understanding that we are dust. "Your will be done <u>in Earth</u> as it is <u>In Heaven</u>."

What this tells me is that I can have the Kingdom NOW, the Kingdom Authority Now, the Kingdom Benefits Now, the Kingdom Deliverance Now, and Kingdom Healing Now. So many times, so many of us are waiting for the Afterlife to acquire the Kingdom when Jesus came to give us the "Kingdom Now Life!"

I learned recently that an animal known as the African impala has the ability to jump from a standstill to thirteen feet in the air, without breaking a sweat. Even though they are able to do this and achieve such great heights, when kept in captivity, zoo-keepers learned that they only need three-foot-high fences to keep them in because the impala will not jump if they cannot see where they will land. Isn't that often how people are? ***Couldn't it be said that we often lack the faith we need to act on what God is calling us to do?***

Even though God has equipped us to "jump" by the power of His Spirit and for the purpose of making Kingdom impacts as mentioned throughout the New Testament Church. Jesus has been so clear — we owe it to ourselves and each other to challenge ourselves to jump with the eyes of faith!

> *Jesus said, Come. And when Peter was come down out of the ship, he walked on the water, to go to Jesus.*
> (Matthew 14:29)

    I have heard many sermons about Peter the Apostle stepping out or "leaping out on nothing" and I do agree that in the natural, there was nothing but strong, raging waves and wind beating against Peter's brow. But upon closer look at the scripture I find that Peter did step out on something – something very sure and stable - THE WORD!

    Jesus spoke the word "Come" and Peter's Kingdom reply was, "Lord if you want me to come, I will step out on your Word, C-O-M-E."

    I know he began to sink, but let's hand it to Peter – he was the ONLY one out there on the water - the others remained on the ship. You may not quite get my point, so please let me attempt to make it more easily understood. If God speaks a Word to you, although the odds may be against you, though it may appear that you have nothing to work with or walk on, if you step out on that Word, Christ will never let you down. Step out by faith, do something others have told you was impossible. Step out on that Word that is spelled C-O-M-E. After all, the worst

NOVEMBER 5 — RECYCLED BY GRACE

case scenario is that you would be reaching up to a hand reaching down to you. Jesus will save you. He's got your back!

I believe it is time for God's people to take some big steps by faith, forsaking form and religion, seeking the supernatural. Perhaps as you read this book, you too will receive an invitation to the supernatural. Jesus saves us by empowering us to move out of sin, to begin to live for God and live free from sin. In that way He is doing something **big** in our lives.

My life had become trash because I was in bondage to the enemy of my soul; but I was delivered and experienced the Kingdom. Many of us today have a life that seems so void and numb, becoming trash right before our eyes.

We aren't getting our lives and the source of life from God. We're trying to get our lives and validation from our work, or a savings account, or from relationships with friends or lovers. Let's be real, we've all tried to gauge our success in life through a lot of other things.

But Jesus desires us to experience His validation, knowing that our worth and our significance come from the Creator, not His creation.

> ***Our worth and our significance must come from the Creator, and not His creation!***

Some of us have had trashy lives because of addictions. Not just addictions to drugs or alcohol, but addiction to work, to pornography, sex, or even to religion, thinking we could earn God's love. However, Jesus on the cross at Calvary showed us that we don't **need** to earn God's love, it is already there waiting for us to receive and embrace it. Having received and embraced His love, He forgives our sins and empowers us to begin a life in accord with His will, as rightly related to others. To some degree, our lives have all been trashed by the things that divide us: not being able to relate to people of a different race, or a different gender, or nationality, or economic status.

The enemy was making trash of humanity in general. However, Jesus has a Recycling by Grace Experience for each of us! The Bible says He came and He made one new humanity. When He died on the cross, He tore down all those frivolous, stupid walls that we set up, and created a Kingdom, a community of people – a new humanity who in Christ simply don't give any significance to the distinctions on race, nationality, etc., which empowers us to rightly relate to all people at all times. When we do this, we are empowered to live in constant dynamic change, bringing the Kingdom to the here-and-now instead of the sweet-by-and-by!

He empowers us to live a Kingdom Way of living where our confidence is no longer based on flexing our muscle over others but rather in serving others.

It's a towel-washing kind of power, where we wash the feet of even our enemies and know the hope of the world lies in that. In doing that, living in us and creating that character, Jesus Christ is turning our trash into something beautiful that is fit for the Kingdom. Some of us believed our lives were trash because the world had afflicted us with so many wounds and scars. We were afflicted with depression, fears, hopelessness, and all sorts of emptiness. Our lives appeared useless, but Jesus has a Recycling by Grace Experience for each of us! God desires to share His joy, His peace, and His life with us. In so doing, He shares His future with us.

NOVEMBER 5 — RECYCLED BY GRACE

So, where once we were fearful, we can now shine with boldness; and though we were in despair, there can now be joy; and where there was anxiety, now there can be peace, and a multitude of others things called the fruit of the Spirit.

God is in the process of transforming us — once fit only for the trash bin. He's saving through his Recycle by Grace Experience, making us fit for the Kingdom. He is bringing wholeness into our lives, restoring us not only as a nation, but as humanity.

That is the theme of this book – He is conforming us to the beautiful image of Jesus Christ. **He is making us beautiful reflections of himself, fit for the Kingdom!**

Focusing exclusively on a "legal transaction" that cancels Hell completely misses the point. It certainly misses all the good stuff. It's like saying that the point of going to high school is to find a loophole so you don't flunk out your senior year. Really, is that the point of going to high school? No. The point of going to school is to learn, and become a certain kind of person who is ready to meet the world and apply what's been learned. If you do that, you will manage not to flunk your senior year in high school. But if you go into it thinking the goal is to find a loophole to keep you from flunking, what's going to happen is that you're not going to learn what you're supposed to learn, or grow the way that you're supposed to grow, and the school will not be doing what it's supposed to do to prepare you for your future.

It's the same with salvation; the point of salvation is not to find a loophole, a way for trash to escape from being thrown where trash belongs.

The point is: *If we allow God to recycle us through His grace, we will be transformed out of our trash, becoming a person fit for the Kingdom rather than the trash bin.*

God loves transforming trash into testimonies of redemption, and taking ugly stuff and turning it into beautiful stuff and beautiful people who reflect his character and are fit for the Kingdom – that is salvation! That's the Biblical view of salvation. It's holistic, it's broad, it's beautiful, and it encompasses everything. ***This is what it means to belong to the Kingdom.***

CHAPTER 12

My Recycled Life

Leonard Cohen said, "Children show scars like medals. Lovers use them as secrets to reveal. A scar is what happens when the word is made flesh."

He is not here: for He is risen, as He said. Come; see the place where the Lord lay.

(Mathew 28:6)

If you think about a grave or a cemetery, you usually think of a place of grief, of death and mourning. It's a place of hopelessness, is it not? Finality! Yes, death is an ending to something, but the resurrection wasn't the end of the life of Christ; rather, it was the beginning of His life in the church. When Mary went to Jesus' gravesite to mourn and lament, she received an announcement that blew her mind. An angel of the Lord tells her there is nothing to weep about in this place anymore. This place that was thought to represent death, now actually represents new life. **Your NEW LIFE!**

I would like to share with you the amazing concept that every place of death has the potential to be turned into a place of life. Every place of sorrow has the potential to be turned into gladness. Every ending can really be a beginning — just as what seems like a caterpillar's ending is actually the start of its transformation into a beautiful butterfly!

This is why the angels said, behold this place that you've seen through the eyes of sorrow, you shall now see it as a place of great joy.

What is that place you go to in your mind, in your heart and emotions that is a place of tragedy and sorrow? A place where you thought your life was over?

A life being lived on a, "November 4 day," a day of loneliness, failures, addiction and desperation. A day that has only darkness with no light in sight…I have an announcement for you — your "Recycled by Grace" Experience is on its way!

Let me explain what's happening right now. Sorrow is being broken over your life.

I speak this by the authority and the anointing of Jesus Christ!

They thought they were seeing a ghost or spirit and Jesus said to them, "Behold my hands and behold my feet." It was at that moment that they looked at those hands and they fell on their knees and said, "Master." They knew that it was Jesus.

See my hands and my feet, that it is truly me. Touch me and see, for a spirit doesn't have flesh and bones, as you see that I have.
(Luke 24:39)

RECYCLED BY LIFE

The world in which we live just may come to know the true people of God by the scars that we bear. I heard a preacher not long ago say he was selling a book called "No More Scars." When I saw that, I thought to myself, "If God didn't take the scars and the marks away from His Son's hands; He'll never take them away from His body, the church. No, those wounds were not bleeding anymore, but the marks were still on His hands; the holes were still in His feet."

Why? Because what you've been through is the identification for the world to recognize what's in you. I remember a few months ago a man began to share with me how he felt that I was a poor leader and that my life had suffered many setbacks and failures. He said, "Shane you have a lot of scars don't you my friend?" I answered him saying, *"When I stand before you, yes, you will see my scars, and know that I have had my wars. I suffered many wounds **but I also experienced many healings**. God brought me through it all."*

We have been taught by professional preachers, not anointed ones, how to cover our scars – to cover our past and "be healed from it." I say to you that that's one of the biggest lies that the devil will ever tell you. Don't hide the marks of your suffering because those scars just might be the thing that causes people to know Jesus in you.

I read in the Bible that we as God's people overcame by the blood of the Lamb and the word of our testimony. We will, in fact, have scars, but that is what helps us to overcome, and show others that we are the victors!

"Behold my hands, behold my feet." When they saw that, they knew that there was only one who had suffered for their transgressions, died, and then resurrected. There was only one that hung on that tree for the sins of mankind. No longer were they hearing a big tall tale; they knew without a shadow of doubt. **He's alive.**

Christ showed them His hands and His feet as if to say, "Look here now, the cross had me but could not hold me, the grave tried to snatch me but could not steal me; oh yeah it looked fatal but it was not final, I was wounded but I am the winner!"

As a believer, I have one job and that is to testify of Him. I learned to stop trying to get people cleaned up. Stop trying to debate and correct everyone. ***Just begin to testify.***

I've been with Him. I've seen Him, I've touched Him, I felt Him, I know Him. Jesus describes our lives in the Kingdom as dying to ourselves. It feels like death. If you're willing to die, you'll live. That's the payoff.

> *He that findeth his life shall lose it: and he that loseth his life for my sake shall find it.*
>
> (Mathew 10:39)

That's the Kingdom Principle. It means saying no to some of the things you'd want to say yes to. It means you don't get to make all your own decisions. You submit everything to Him. It means that you subject your aspirations to Him and everything you're about to Him.

It requires you to say no to yourself, but the payoff is worth it. It's a life principle; the Calvary principle — no pain, no gain.

What's happening as you read the closing words of this book

right now? No matter who you are, where you are at, or what you've done, I have prayed over these writings and God spoke to my spirit: He will minister to all of those who read this book and open their hearts to receive of the Lord! He's beginning to show up.

There's nothing that will keep Him away from you right now. It is with great confidence that I say these words to you **"Behold Him!"**

May I draw your attention to the fact that it was only after Thomas reached out and felt the wounds of the body of Christ that he was truly able to understand who Christ really was!

There are many groups of people in the world today that consistently go to church, meet in a building, reach out for each other's fellowship, having never reached out to feel the wounds of the body of Christ! When you feel the wounds of His body, you will better understand who He really is.

CHAPTER 13

Kingdom Keys

At the time of writing this book, I have had the awesome privilege of traveling to all but a handful of states, preaching over 5,000 sermons in various churches, over the course of 20 years. God has given me the gift of reaching millions through revivals, camp meetings, conferences, television, radio, and the Internet. I am so thankful to God. Perhaps you are asking, "How can I be of use to God like that?" Let me assure you that you can be a great champion for the Kingdom of God without ever stepping on a church platform or standing behind a pulpit or podium.

I want to bring a Kingdom example to the forefront of your thinking. Many people will be surprised that I am using an example of someone they have never heard of, or ever considered as being a Kingdom Champion!

I did not choose a well-know biblical hero, such as Samson, King David, Solomon, The Apostle Peter, Paul, Timothy, or James, because if I did, one may conclude that to work for the Kingdom, and truly be a champion of faith, one would need to be like Samson and tie some fox tails together, or be like David and have mighty victories over lions and bears, or write a great book as Paul did, or have the faith, strength and boldness of Peter, stepping out onto the raging waters to walk towards Jesus.

However, to be of great use to God, you do not have to accomplish something great or be measured by anyone else's notion of what a Kingdom Champion should be. I am going to tell you about a great hero of God, a great Kingdom worker, who had great Kingdom impact without really ever leaving the house! I have your attention now, don't I?

THE GOSPEL OF ANNA ~ NYMITY

Anonymity: when a person's name and other personally identifying information is not known.

Example – The man who gave a large donation chose anonymity.

Anna, a prophetess, and daughter of Phanuel of the tribe of Asher, is the person I have chosen to write about. Most people, even within the community of faith, have no idea who she is, yet Anna demonstrated the Kingdom of God on a daily basis. Anna lived with her husband seven years after their marriage and then was a widow until she was 84, which is when this passage happens.

> *Anna had been a widow for eighty-four years; she was in the Temple at all times, worshipping with prayers and going without food, night and day.*
>
> *(Luke 2:37)*

Anna probably married when she was around thirteen. Her husband died seven years later, when she was around twenty. So, for 64 years or so, this lady, Anna had been in the temple worshipping, fasting and praying, and remaining dedicated to God.

GOD DESIRES TO USE US RIGHT WHERE WE ARE

Anna was a woman used by God to prophesy, which is speaking the Word of God authoritatively, under the inspiration of the Holy Spirit, to whoever is listening, including both men and women. God's desire is for all people, women and men, to operate out of their giftedness and their calling; no walls are put up on who can or cannot be used of God. The Kingdom is not a place where customary social barriers and restrictions apply.

God does not necessarily look at one's ability. Rather, He looks at one's availability. Anna is a beautiful picture of the Kingdom because she had this incredible life that was lived almost entirely in solitude.

For 64 years this woman stayed in the Temple building and although she may have had a residence where she slept, bathed and ate, her life was basically spent inside of the walls of the Temple; and all she did there was worship and fast, and when the Holy Spirit came on her, she prophesied. When they had services in the Temple and the priest would offer sacrifices and go through protocol, Anna was right there in the front row. The people of the town knew she would be there regardless of what was going on outside the Temple. Anna had no extraordinary gifts that we know about. She wasn't a teacher who impacted the world or made a great impression on anyone. She never went into politics or wrote a book or did anything that by the world's standards would be considered successful or making a difference.

In fact, in all probability, as a Jewish woman in the first century, she was probably uneducated and unable to read or write. Yet the woman in this passage is highlighted as being a hero. Because she was a hero, a success in God's eyes, God blesses her by allowing her to be one of the few people to have their eyes opened to see the Christ child being born in this world; and one of the very few blessed to be part of the inauguration of this wonderful Kingdom movement.

Anna would not be a hero by any ordinary standards of the world.

In fact, by contemporary standards, we may be inclined to see her life as being rather boring and pathetic. I mean, how sad, how tragic is this woman, who was alone all that time in the Temple and did nothing with her life? She didn't participate in society or know the joys of raising children or having a lifelong mate. Our contemporary heroes aren't like Anna, are they? If we imagine a winner and a great Kingdom Victor, Anna would not be what we would picture.

Our heroes are people who are get their faces on *Time* or *Cosmopolitan* magazine or win *American Idol*; or the movers and shakers who make an impact, but not necessarily for the good. If a person happens to be equipped with the right talent, the right personality, the right voice or athletic gifts, they qualify as heroes. That is where our culture is, and I don't think it's really that much different in religious circles. We have our heroes in religious circles, too – people with super personalities who have the charisma to pack auditoriums and impress crowds. They write books that sell millions. There's just something exceptional about them. We tend to think, "Oh, they are so used by God, and so close to

God, their prayers must count more than my prayers; there is a special anointing on their lives." In other words, we tend to spiritualize the world's criteria of success and choose heroes by the world's standards. We need to see that God doesn't think the way we do. His criteria standards for success are not contemporary society's criteria for success! God is looking for people that have the Anna-nymity mindsets.

Anna was an avid worshipper, which tells us something about the Body of Christ, and Christ Himself!

THE KEY OF WORSHIP

The Kingdom that Anna is helping to inaugurate is centered on worship. That is why we, as Kingdom People, must put a high priority on true worship. Worship is our pipeline, our umbilical cord to the Almighty, if you will. Here is where the life of God just flows into us! Anna is a hero for one reason, and one reason only – because she was exactly where God called her to be, nothing more, nothing less. She obeyed the Lord and she is a hero because, you see, God is, so to speak, an odd God. If God doesn't seem odd to you, you are not thinking accurately about Him. When you understand God and the Kingdom, your natural suppositions about everything will be turned inside out and upside down. The "wow people" actually turn out to be the least, and the "not well-known people" the greatest. Those who serve are greater than those who are waited on. The first shall be last and the last shall be first. Everything is upside down.

If you have a nice yacht or you are successful by the world's standard, there is nothing wrong with that; bless you for it.

If that's your gift, use it for the Kingdom. What you do with it, how you obey God, how you walk with God, that is what matters. Fame and fortune are utterly irrelevant to God. What matters is not who knows you, but does God know you and vice versa? Are you walking in faithfulness to him? By this standard, Anna was a stellar success.

> *She may even be one of the greatest heroes in all of Kingdom history!*

Are you seeking first the Kingdom of God? Are you doing what God calls you to do? If you are, it really doesn't matter who knows it, or who doesn't know it; it doesn't matter how the world measures it. All that matters is that you do what God calls you to do. I want us to become like Anna. God raised up this verse in Acts 10:38, where it says, "God anointed Jesus of Nazareth to go about doing good." It is that simple. By doing good, you are freeing people from darkness, fear and oppression.

The full thrust of the anointing of the Kingdom, the whole plan of salvation, can be summarized by this incredibly simple phrase – **do good**.

Just do good and serve. Listen to God and go where He leads and guides you to be, just do that. So, when they asked, "Lord how do you want us to serve?" He gave them a wonderful analogy in Anna. Just open your eyes and simply serve; start coming with the determination to serve and help others. Then, when the time is right, **then** you share the good news of Jesus Christ. But don't do it in order to gain "spiritual superiority." That is what many Christians do!

We do a good deed, but then, it is like, "Now I believe in Jesus; now I can sign on the dotted line." We should never try to help or speak into someone's life for an ulterior reason — like wanting them to agree with our theology. *You should do a good deed because it is a good deed and the right, Kingdom thing to do!*

I remember in the first year we pastored, a married couple approached us seeking approval to use our church's name as they went throughout the community performing random acts of kindness, exemplifying the love of Christ. When I inquired as to their plans, I was shocked to hear what their desire for Kingdom work was – this couple wanted to visit various gas stations around the city armed with a janitorial-looking basket of cleaning items. They would ask the attendant or the cashier if they could do a random act of kindness and clean that business' bathrooms, free of charge.

They would do this with no strings attached, because of God's goodness in their lives and their desire to do good for others. Of course, I had never heard of such Kingdom work, and was blown away with the love of God that this couple demonstrated.

When the church secretary and youth pastor heard the idea, they responded, "I ain't gonna clean no filthy bathroom." That may be the reader's response right now, too.

Perhaps the problem in today's churches is that, in fact, we have many youth pastors but not enough people truly reaching out to the youth! We have people who hold church titles but do not possess a humble spirit to serve. They may want their name outside their office, or a nice desk, or may love doing the church's books, but just not clean a bathroom?

Kingdom work happens when you leave the world a better place, whatever happens.

You are expanding the love of Jesus Christ, whether they end up agreeing with your theology or not. Every day ask the question: "How can I serve?"

> **"What good thing can I do?"**
> *This is an Anna mentality, driven by Anna~nymity.*

You don't necessarily need to strategize how to have an impact. The question isn't how can I be successful by the world's standards, but rather, how can I be faithful? Faithfulness is always about service, in whatever form it takes. Trust that God is working in people's lives. The criteria of our success should be this - are we cooperatively doing what Jesus did on the cross when He died for those who were crucifying Him?

What really excites me as a Kingdom worker is when I hear about somebody who decides to give up a Saturday morning and help serve in a homeless shelter or soup line.

I love to hear about people volunteering a few hours a week to help children at youth centers across America. The faith based community stepping into action to help inner-city kids learn to read, or when I hear about people who feel led to adopt children, giving them a better life. Doing their best to assure their salvation! I love it when I hear, read, or get involved with others performing random acts of kindness, not as a setup to invite them to a church, but rather to bring the church to them. That makes me want to dance. That is the Kingdom going on!

That is the Kingdom of God because it looks like Jesus Christ. What matters is that you walk with your eyes open and think, "What good thing can I do? What good word can I say? How can I serve the world around me?"

> **The Anna question is simply this: "Lord,**
> **how would you have me serve?"**

God will tell you, He will put it on your heart. It doesn't matter if it is a big thing or a little thing. How you serve God is every bit as important as how anyone else out there serves God. If you are doing what God calls you to do, drink deeply of the satisfaction of a job well done. Do not measure success by the world's standards; God measure success by faithfulness. Take whatever it is God calls you to do, do it with passion and be satisfied with it. Stay open to how God will lead you to do it.

*What I see in this Anna~nymity principle is —
don't strive for success, strive for service!*

THE KEY OF "RELATIONSHIP," NOT A RELIGION

The second principal of Anna is this: an Anna Christian cultivates a private relationship with God. Anna had a private, personal relationship with God – God was real to her.

If God hadn't been real to her it would have been torture for her, would it not? Many modern people would look at her life and think it would be terrible. **All she had was God.**

But, I don't think she was really lonely. There may have been times of doubt, but God was real to her. *God was her best friend. God was her companion!*

God was a reality to her. She talked to God and worshipped God and obeyed God all day long. I can imagine Anna having more joy and more peace and more authority in the spiritual realm than many of us dream about.

This brings up the importance of the solitude, the aloneness, the secrecy and the hiddeness of Anna, as a Kingdom Person. The only way to cultivate a sense of God's reality and a genuine transforming relationship with God is by having private time with God. You must carve out a space in your busy life where you are disciplined about having alone time with God. It is so easy, in our day and age, to have our relationship with God be defined by externals, by what we do in public. We think about God when we are at church, but otherwise we don't; we pray at church when everyone is praying, but otherwise we don't; we read the Bible with everyone else at church, but otherwise we don't, and so our relationship with God is defined publicly.

However, we've got to carve out some private time with the Lord.

The only way to cultivate a sense of God's reality, and a genuine transforming Relationship with God, is by having quality, private time with God!

I sincerely believe this; some of us are dealing with issues that would largely disappear if we simply carved out more time to be alone with God.

GOD'S NOT MAD AT YA!

I recently had the honor of meeting a very special young man named Ken. We went to church together recently, and on the way Ken made a statement that really blew me away. He had heard a minister teaching the night before. He described this man's ministry by saying, "Shane, this preacher really convinced me that God wasn't mad at me!" I thought about this simple, yet powerful, statement. When I began comparing it to scripture, the accounts given in the Bible, this statement impacted me greatly. The Bible teaches that if we are to learn about God and how He would respond to any given situation, all we must do is open the pages of the Bible and look at Jesus Christ!

Hebrews 1:3 teaches us that Jesus is the "express image" of God. In other words, Jesus Christ, in His humanity, perfectly mirrors God. Just as someone who holds up a mirror to their face would see a "perfect reflection" of themselves in that mirror, therefore if we want to know what God looks like, what He thinks, how He acts, or even God's point of view on any given subject, all that we have to do is look at Jesus! What did He say? How did He act and respond? What was His point of view on the subject?

On the way home from church that night, I told my friend Ken, pointing him to the scriptures, that Jesus never got mad at a SINNER! He never turned away someone in need or condemned a person he found in sin, yet were repentant and asking forgiveness. Two examples come to mind: the woman found in the "act of adultery," and the wild demon-possessed man who was the first noted "cutter," who harmed himself with sharp stones and rocks.

Jesus never got mad at souls who acknowledged themselves as sinners. The downcast and downtrodden are the ones that Christ accepted so freely. The ones Jesus had a problem with were the religious sects – people going around trying to merit salvation with their good works and fine speech. They had the look and the talk, but they had no humble walk. Instead of establishing a relationship with God, they were pulled down and drowning in the quicksand of religious mindsets and self-righteousness.

You cannot find one place in scripture that gives an account of Jesus getting mad at someone who had fallen down, been tormented, or cast out.

In fact, these are the ones that Jesus said He came for! He declared to the crowds, "the whole need no physician."

To the unbeliever who may be reading this, or the one who is, perhaps, away from God right now, and in need of prayer, or a breakthrough, because you think that God is mad at you — hear this: **God's not mad at ya!**

In closing this book I am feeling like the evangelist I have been for nearly twenty years, reaching out to the one who is hurting, the one who is wounded, the one that may be wondering about their relationship between themselves and God.

CHAPTER 14

Closing Thoughts

The Bible talks about salvation in three tenses, past, present and future.

The Apostle Paul says for example in Ephesians 2, "God made us alive with Christ when we were dead in transgressions. It is by grace you have **been saved**." Past tense, we have been saved. When you surrendered your life to Christ, you were saved, past tense. But it also talks about salvation in the present tense. Did you ever notice that? For example, in 1 Corinthians 1, Paul says "For the message of the cross is foolishness to those who are perishing, but to us who are **being saved** it is the power of God." To those who are in the process of being saved, that's an interesting thing. We don't talk about that very much around the church. We always say, or ask, "Are you saved?" We don't say or ask, "Are you in the process of being saved?" The Bible does.

The Bible also talks about salvation in the future tense. Romans Chapter 5 says, "For if, when we were God's enemies, we were reconciled to Him through the death of His Son, how much more, having been reconciled, **shall we be saved** through

His life." Future tense — I have been saved, I am being saved, I shall be saved.

The reason we don't talk that way very much in our church circles anymore is because we have a courtroom analogy, and this thinking governs our whole thought process about salvation.

In the courtroom analogy it makes no sense to talk that way. You either signed the deal or you didn't, it's either a legal transaction or it's not. But if you think more in terms of Covenant, it makes perfect sense. **I was married, I am being married, I shall be married.**

It's a relationship that occurs over time. I was saved when I first surrendered my life and made Jesus Christ my Lord and Savior, and at that time it's as if God says, "Okay great, now I got something I can work with. I can plant my seed into Shane's life and 'Recycle' him, bringing a Kingdom work through and in him." *God basically says, I can start to clean the garage out!*

But I'm also being saved because the garbage is still being taken out in a definite, yet progressive way, and I shall be saved because when all the garbage is taken out, then the light of truth will manifest greatly in my life, and it will be clear that I am in fact, fit for the Kingdom. God has "Recycled" me, and made me fit for the Kingdom. All three tenses apply.

Justification is a word that when I first began meeting different church people, I heard quite often, now it seems that the word justification has long been forgotten, or at least by my past circles of church fellowship and ministries. The word means "declared righteous." We are declared righteous. Unfortunately, when God said, "Let Shane West be righteous," there was something that resisted it, something that fought, and even today fights back constantly, pushes and pulls back and forth, like a tug of war. It's the old Shane West, it's the trashy Shane West and now my whole life is about living the truth of who I am, because

CLOSING THOUGHTS

of what God has done, what He is doing, and what He will continue to do!

Our only job is to yield to what God is doing to fulfill His greatness in our lives.

What Paul says throughout his writings is simply this…take out the trash, it's not who you really are. You have been justified, you are being justified, and you shall be justified. So get rid of all the trash that disagrees with this simple truth, because in fact you are a holy creature in Christ Jesus, you are righteous in Christ Jesus, you are a child of God in Christ Jesus!

Do not lend an ear to "Trash Talking" of the enemy. Ignore it - get rid of that trash-thinking process! Get rid of those trashy emotions, that trashy attitude and behavior that you acquired in life. We need to quit acting, thinking and feeling like trash, and manifest our new selves in Christ Jesus. This is who you truly are! We are "Recycled by Grace." No pretending here, God does see the trash, and still He loves us. *What we often see and focus our attentions on is not what we are destined to be!*

The question is will you agree with Him? Will we allow Him to reign over us with Kingdom Thinking and Kingdom living?

Many church goers may attend Easter and Christmas services, and they may even pray once in awhile when they're in trouble, but otherwise they have no implications of Kingdom living in their life. That's not a relationship. That's not Covenant, that's not a marriage.

When I got married, when I pledged verbally my life's dedication to my wife, my pledge was not in words only, but rather my life, dedication, and heart was committed that day. The quality of my marriage is not determined by the fact, that I "once upon a time" pledged my life and heart to my wife Dana, but rather the quality of my marriage is determined by living the life that I pledged to give her. So the question is not did I pledge my life 20 years ago, but am I living out that pledge in my life now? Am I living out that pledge? Am I surrendering this moment to her? The only life I have to give my wife is the life I'm living right now. I'm in the now. It's the same thing in our relationship with Christ.

It's wonderful that once upon a time we surrendered our hearts and lives to Christ. That was a good start, but the quality of that commitment is determined by what we do with our lives now, today, the real life that we live moment by moment. So the important question is not, did you surrender your life to Christ 20 years ago or 40 years ago, but are you surrendering your life to Christ right now, today?

The only life we have to surrender is the one we're living at this very moment, and now **IS the moment**.

Jesus wants to be Lord in our lives, and that means Lord of this moment, the whole moment, this "now moment", because the only life I've got is this one right here, and right now. Because of our surrendered life to Christ and because of the finished work He did at Calvary, we are fit for the Kingdom, and all that Kingdom living has to offer. No matter the age, the nationality, the background, poor or rich, God desires to impact us with Kingdom Living!

The reality is that many lives have become or are currently headed toward becoming trash because of our bondage to sin. Bondage is simply anything that can separate us from God.

But Jesus saves us and delivers us by bringing about forgiveness for sins. But, He also saves us by *empowering* us by living in and through us; by bringing the Kingdom and impacting the lives of those who encounter Christ!

You may believe as did the man in the scripture who cried out, "God I am not worthy of anything, have pity on me."

CLOSING THOUGHTS

I am reaching out to you with this simple truth: If you will believe the Word of God with me and embrace the Biblical fact that Jesus Christ is the "perfect expression" of God Almighty, then you can believe me when I tell you that *"God's love is here for you right now!"*

If you are down, let Christ pick you back up!

The LORD is nigh unto them that are of a broken heart; and saveth such as be of a contrite spirit.
(Psalm 34:18)

God is close to you right now. Reach out to Him as He is reaching out to you!

Do you remember reading a few pages back, the time that God spoke to my heart and made me the amazing promise that if I would follow Him, He would show me what peace and happiness was really all about? He has kept His promise! He will keep His promises.

I have a Heavenly Father that loves, cares, protects, guides, and provides for me, Shane West, a piece of trash that God reached down and recycled by His Grace. That same Grace is reaching you through this book right now.

Please accept it and be blessed!

RECYCLED BY GRACE

Allow God to "Recycle us by His Grace."

Amazing Grace, how sweet the sound,
That saved a wretch like me....
I once was lost but now am found,
Was blind, but now, I see.

T'was Grace that taught...
my heart to fear.
And Grace, my fears relieved.
How precious did that Grace appear...
the hour I first believed.

Through many dangers, toils and snares...
we have already come.
T'was Grace that brought us safe thus far...
and Grace will lead us home.

The Lord has promised good to me...
His word my hope secures.
He will my shield and portion be...
as long as life endures.

Yea, when this flesh and heart shall fail,
and mortal life shall cease,
I shall possess within the veil,
a life of joy and peace.

CLOSING THOUGHTS

When we've been here ten thousand years...
bright shining as the sun.
We've no less days to sing God's praise...
then when we've first begun.

Amazing Grace, how sweet the sound,
That saved a wretch like me....
I once was lost but now am found,
Was blind, but now, I see.